Democratization in the Balkans

Democratization in the Balkans

Prescription for a Badly Scarred Body Politic

Richard P. Farkas

Northeastern University Press
Boston
Published by University Press of New England
Hanover and London

Northeastern University Press
Published by University Press of New England,
One Court Street, Lebanon, NH 03766
www.upne.com
© 2007 by Northeastern University Press
Printed in the United States of America
5 4 3 2 1

Library of Congress Cataloging-in-Publication Data
Farkas, Richard P.
Democratization in the Balkans : prescription for a badly scarred body politic / Richard P. Farkas.
    p.   cm. — (Northeastern series on democratization and political development)
Includes bibliographical references and index.
ISBN-13: 978–1–55553–690–9 (cloth : alk. paper)
ISBN-10: 1–55553–690–5 (cloth : alk. paper)
ISBN-13: 978–1–55553–691–6 (pbk. : alk. paper)
ISBN-10: 1–55553–691–3 (pbk. : alk. paper)
1. Balkan Peninsula—Politics and government—1989– 2. Democracy—Balkan Peninsula.
3. Post-communism—Balkan Peninsula. I. Title.
DR48.6.F37 2007
320.9496—dc22   2007025946

 University Press of New England is a member of the Green Press Initiative.
The paper used in this book meets their minimum requirements for
recycled paper.

To Eric and Andre—two men whose

courage, energy, and resilience are inspirational

and to Anne and Amy who recruited them

into our family

Contents

Acknowledgments

It is with sincere appreciation that I acknowledge the professionalism and input of University Press of New England and the contributions of M. Ellen Wicklum, Bill Crotty, Betty Waterhouse, Cecile Regner, Valerie Paulson, Bill Goodman and Bekim Rakoci to this volume.

Abbreviations

BBC	British Broadcasting Company
BiH	Bosnia and Hercegovina
DS	Democratic Party (Serbia)
EU	European Union
FBH	Federation of Muslims and Croatians
IDEA	International Institute for Democracy and Electoral Assistance
KLA	Kosovar Liberation Army (in Albanian "UCK")
KTA	Kosovo Trust Agency
LDK	Democratic League of Kosovo
MPC	Macedonian Orthodox Church
NATO	North Atlantic Treaty Organization
NGO	non-governmental organization
OPTOR	Serbian NGO of Serbian youth against Milosevic ("resist")
ORA	"Time" (political party in Kosovo)
SAA	Stabilization and Association Agreement
SDS	Democratic Party of Serbia
SNSD	Alliance of Independent Social Democrats (Serbia)
SPC	Serbian Orthodox Church
SR	Srpska Republic
TV CG	Television Cena Gora (Montenegro)
U.N.	United Nations
UNMIK	United Nations Mission in Kosovo
VAT	value added tax

Democratization in the Balkans

Introduction

Throughout most of the twentieth century, one political system stood in sharp contrast to the others in the world. Four generations of American and global leaders contended with images and stereotypes of the so-called communist political systems. Communist political systems claimed a distinct ideological heritage, a contrasting goal culture (what societies say they want to achieve), a different institutional structure (how governing is organized), and a pattern of political behaviors (mass and elite) unlike other political systems in history. In many ways, that legacy is what makes the former communist countries such interesting cases for contemporary comparative analysis. They share elements of the same recent political heritage and are struggling with what to change and how to change to meet the domestic and international conditions of the twenty-first century.

Accompanying the disintegration and collapse of Soviet-style and Yugoslav-style communism between 1989 and 1992, the fundamental characteristics of the political and economic systems in Southeast Europe changed. All of the ideological conflict and most of the political antagonism stemming from systemic differences between East and West vanished. It is that process and those changes that draw our attention. In comparative politics, it is important to remember that we strive to use social scientific means to examine how systems organize themselves, adapt, and manage. It is also important to remember that, like all living systems, societies can become ill and may even die. In today's language such political systems are called "failed states." Lessons from the communist era in Southeast Europe are instructive in this way. Nonetheless, the larger and more intellectually valuable task is to take a comparative look at the Balkan countries' experiences with transition. Can these countries implement the West's ideological prescriptions? We need to understand the implications. These countries are experiencing a metamorphosis. We know what they looked like; we are observing their transformations. Crucially, we watch as the political leaders outline objectives and try to enlist their publics. Less clear is just how manageable the transition is. Social scientists have recognized that because no political system has ever been through this particular process (that is, from communism to something else), it is an illuminating and instructive political experiment whatever the outcome.

Transition from communism to a new societal template in the Balkans (whatever its ultimate form) is a rare opportunity to observe and assess the issues and influences working on a variety of political systems. Very broadly speaking, the articulated goal of these changes is to establish "democracy" and attendant market economies. For the casual observer, the story stops with the identification of the goal. For scholars, the modern narrative for these societies is just beginning. To underestimate the task is a disservice to our understanding of democracy and, in some ways more consequential, is a disservice to the enormous challenges faced by the societies trying to transition.

The specific effort this volume represents is to share prescriptions for the design and implementation of routines, behaviors, and structures that can support democratic development. If the process is to be genuine, the hurdles are numerous. Many suggestions contained herein prescribe goals; others, mechanisms. Transition of such a fundamental sort requires reworking goals, relationships, behaviors, and modes of management and leadership.

As a general rubric, there are three requisites to creating a viable democracy in the Balkans. First, within each society, a consensus of political *values* must emerge or be created. Second, *political architecture* will need to be designed and refined to create policies and administration for each society. In essence, this architecture will house the processes that must be ongoing in a democratic milieu. Finally, effective *leadership* will need to be identified and empowered with authority. These generic requisites will be developed more thoroughly in terms of their rationale and the role each plays in the transition.

The design of this volume will attempt to examine what "democracy" actually means to the various players in a society—whether those exercising power, those transmitting power through the society, or those impacted by authoritative decisions—in simple terms, how elites and masses understand and behave in a solidifying democracy. I shall gauge the progress by comparing and contrasting the various Balkan postcommunist societies, focusing on those elements that define a functioning democracy: tolerance, obligation, voice, constraint, transparency, and legitimacy. I shall conclude with a forthright, focused sense of what can be expected of democratic development in both the shorter and longer terms. I shall also survey the range of significant factors that can derail such development.

In many cultures, scars are a symbol of toughness, achievement, and maturity. They often represent the travails associated with challenges, watershed transitional moments in a life cycle. They embody a pride often generated by suffering tempered by courage and fortitude. In simple terms, scars are tougher skin that, from its experience, is thicker, less penetrable, unsightly to some, and abnormal. As such, it is harder to change both physically and psychologically. The body politic in the Balkans is clearly marked by scars from many centuries of trial and conflict. To elaborate on all of them would require a voluminous history (which itself would be very controversial). Suffice it to say that the contemporary political societies in Southeast Europe are layered with such memory-bearing scars. In a functional sense, they make pliability and flexibility—that is, the receptiveness and adaptability to change—all the more difficult to engineer.

As suggested, these scars invite memory. This backward-facing propensity creates palpable resistance to those trying to guide the countries of this region through the thicket of transitions leading to democracy. It is certainly the case that political change of any sort and in any direction would similarly be inhibited by these scars. Nonetheless, authoritarian proponents can argue that the past demonstrates the viability of nondemocratic systems while providing no glowing precedent for the more complex and liberal concepts. This argument faces every regime, especially in moments when public policies fail to meet expectations or to approach their designed objectives.

Communist systems created both an elite and a public psychology that viewed the future with anxiety and trepidation (ironic given Marx's vision). The unknowns associated with the future took on a negative hue. The past represented an uneven, if not ugly, picture but it was "spun" in such a way as to provide explanation for problems and failures. The mistakes were rationalized often for political advantage. Historians were trotted out to account for "mistakes" that caused stagnancy and suffering. *Change* seemed not to capture the imagination as it so often does in democratic political systems. Bureaucracy, corruption, immobility, and systemic constraints of all sorts were tolerable *because* they made life predictable. These societies were rigorously patterned and routinized to reinforce social control. The nature of the guarantees built into the functioning socialist systems of the late twentieth century significantly reduced the uncertainty in everyday life. Prices were fixed, supplies were regular (or predictably unavailable), incomes were leveled and stable, patterns of upward mobility were fixed, jobs and homes were deeply rooted. Contrary to popular impressions, communism was stifling because of its penetrating and pervasive routines. Democracy and capitalism, by contrast, enhance change by guaranteeing little and shifting responsibility to the individual's resourcefulness, performance, or lack thereof. Communist economies were largely predicated on other than performance criteria. The contrast between these people-focused characteristics is sharp.

Readers searching for an intimate examination of any of the individual countries of Southeast Europe will be disappointed. This volume is not organized country by country nor does it seek to prioritize the significance of each as an example of democratization generally. Each and every example is significant by the light it casts on the broader developmental pattern. The pivotal nature of the "Yugoslav" experience will naturally draw a great deal of attention in this volume.

In sum, I present a fresh, clean, and clear analysis of democracy as it unfolds in the Balkans, wrinkles notwithstanding. The picture is meant to be realistic and useful beyond the geographic bounds of the analysis. It is crucial that one recognize that different perceptual screens are brought to the concept of democracy by various cultures and opinion-shapers, both within and beyond Southeast Europe. This effort is designed to stand among those visions and to enhance and inform our understanding.

Chapter 1

The Balkans

The term *Balkans* itself is bound to vanish in the haze of twenty-first-century political jargon. It seems that the United Nations and many other international organizations have concluded that "Balkan" has emerged as a negative and prejudicial label, owing in large measure to the conflict, divisiveness, isolation, bureaucracy, and corruption so evident in the history of the region. Even the people of the region use the term to mean backward!

Reputation and Reality: History with or without Democracy

Such an image is ironic, given that one reasonable view of history offers a very different platform. The Ottoman epoch was not a threat to modernization in the region, although it is often represented that way. The Ottomans brought change of a political sort that might well be viewed as the strongest foundation for democratic processes among the regimes from Balkan history. Political features introduced by the Ottoman Turks have been overlooked because the histories have been written and mainstreamed by scholars and chroniclers from the Slavic successor states.

It is intriguing to note *when* these histories choose to "begin" their narratives. Croatians, for example, begin consistently with the seventh century. But this selection conveniently neglects the reality that Slavs were invaders themselves; they did not enter a vacant land. They displaced some peoples and assimilated others. From the seventh century, Croatian historians then regale the various invasions and oppressions of others over "their homeland." The Ottomans, the Hapsburgs, the Hungarians—all manage to be portrayed as inherent aggressors while the Croatians, in this one example, are presumed to have a natural right to the land. Unfortunately, the selective historical memory

Balkan Peninsula. From: **Maps On File, 2007 Edition** by Facts On File. Balkan Peninsula, 1.06. Copyright © 2007 by Facts On File, Inc. Reprinted by permission of publisher.

of the Croats is typical of other Balkan peoples. All the various ethnic nationalities that inhabit Southeast Europe today have conjured similar, poignant stories that validate themselves and invalidate virtually all others.

Without challenging the accuracy of accounts and legends, it seems clear that history does not hold solutions to the challenges that Southeast European countries face today. History is twisted, rife with contradiction, and emotionally charged in the region. As such, it provides few constructive cues to the policies and behaviors that can support democratization. Nationalism in the region (and beyond) has persistently generated xenophobia, border disputes, and racial, ethnic, and religious intolerance. Violence, death, and the threat of those ills have emerged in successive waves over the centuries.

Yet first, a few words about some of the overlooked but positive elements of the region's past. Every epoch has its benefactors and demons, and there *have* been experiences that can be harvested as contributions to a democratizing process. A quick and admittedly less than comprehensive inventory of these values and mechanisms follows.

The Illyrian heritage that lays claim to the geographical territory under discussion may be seen in quite positive ways. The ancient Pelasgians and the Illyrian civilization that succeeded them were deeply rooted in the length and breadth of the Balkans long before Slavic or Turkic peoples entered the picture. Evidence can be found from the tenth century B.C. These were people oriented to the sea and who proved to be skillful sailors. The practical utility for commercial and political development was accompanied by an impressive capacity to spread Illyrian culture and values. The various Illyrian tribes were the first settled dwellers in the space we now call the Balkans, Greece, and Italy.[1]

Pelasgians were responsible for spreading an alphabet to much of the central Mediterranean and beyond the seacoast into continental Europe. They taught many subsequent peoples how to build walls and "work" metals. The Pelasgian leader Thot (Great Father) is said to have ruled Egypt and is further credited with having introduced philosophy to Moses, Pythagorus, and Plato. The word "pharaoh" is drawn from the Illyrian language, meaning "our stock" or our lineage. The names of the descendant peoples we know well from history: Illyrians, Etruscans, and Thracians. Herodotus claimed that the Pelasgians were the original Athenians. As an indicator of social and cultural development, language serves us by providing a traceable trajectory. Illyrians draw their name from the word *lir,* which meant "free" or "place of the free people." This word stem can be found in the Etruscan, Italian, Latin, French, English, Spanish, Romanian, and Portuguese languages. Illyrian tribes proliferated throughout the Mediterranean basin and as far north and east as the Danube River. The names resounded through history: Etruscans (brains), Danuii (separated), Veneti (homeland), Picenes (place of drinking water), Messapi (center), Lydians, and Italics. The Illyrian word for territory is found in Albanian, Latin, Italian, French, English, Romanian, and Hungarian. The word for ship (*ania*) is evident in Etruscan, Albanian, Sanskrit, Hebrew, Persian, Latin, Italian, Spanish, Portuguese, Romanian, and English. All words and places with the suffix "ona" have Pelasgian origin. Aphrodite in Illyrian means "little girls born early in the morning." "Celt" means clear complexion and "balta" means mud.

The essence of these notions is not to debate any of the particular claims. It is to establish that the indigenous societies were historically and culturally significant, providing antecedents for contemporary ideas. They were in the vanguard of political and economic development. The stellar feature of Illyrian society was the education system. Just as nineteenth-century Europe and twentieth-century America have become the destinations of choice for elites and aspiring elites in those epochs, in the Mediterranean world for a thousand years, such persons made their way to the Balkans. They did this to elevate their cultural prowess, advance their formal education and to establish commercial relationships. Prominent examples include Julius Caesar, Octavian Augustus, and legions of Ottoman leaders. Illyrians themselves rose to positions of immense power—among them Diocletian (255–313 A.D.), Constantine the Great (274–337 A.D.) and Justinian the Great (482–565 A.D.). The emphasis on education and language is reflected in the modern Albanian word that they use to describe themselves—"Shqip"—which literally means "good pronunciation" or "original language speakers." These societies flourished by commerce and reputation. They also developed a record of piracy on the Adriatic Sea.[2] In the third century B.C., the system boasted a female leader, and during its era of greatest unity and influence, women were afforded "equal" rights and real access to education. In relative terms, and in context, it was the enlightened society of its day.

These are mere threads of history in which Balkan peoples could, but rarely do, take pride. The end of their visibility came in 168 B.C., when Illyrians and Macedonians fought and lost to the Romans. Rome divided Illyria into three parts and the groups never again united. Many Illyrian elites fled to Venice, where vestiges of Illyrian culture can still be found, especially in the maritime culture. The Illyrians that found themselves in the Ottoman-ruled part of the Balkans had no trouble establishing themselves as worthy leaders. No fewer than thirty-six grand viziers (Ottoman prime ministers) were of Illyrian heritage. The salient notion here is that the Illyrian societies warrant recognition as perhaps the original Balkan people (at least with a semblance of societal organization), whose energy and achievements need to stand alongside those Romans, Slavs, Ottomans, Venetians, and French who come along later.

Roman experiences in the Balkans suggest that they had an abiding appreciation for the advanced nature of some of the aspects of Balkan life and organization. The Romans brought an elaborately organized and militarized system of governing to the Balkans and elsewhere. As they approached "other peoples," the Romans first offered alliance arrangements; if rejected, they proceeded to conquer the population. Roman imagery and power were projected by the "legions" of Rome. Roman civilization has been sufficiently chronicled, but it is valuable to observe that they were more clearly adept at *manifesting* high culture than they were at creating it. They absorbed much of what they encountered culturally and added one very curious political innovation: they consistently built settlements in duplicate. That is, they constructed one settlement for the civilian population and a second nearby exclusively for the military contingent. These were largely self-sufficient and were purposefully kept apart. The political thinking was that civilians and their ideas and behaviors would contaminate the military if allowed to mingle. Military discipline was paramount and separate settlements were a way of preserving that discipline. The Romans' control of the Balkans was complete with the seizing of the city-state of Ragusa (today Dubrovnik). It stood as the last independent city-state until its conquest by Rome.

The Slavs in various but consistently small numbers seeped into the Balkans from the north. Most histories suggest that these were "land people" from Galicia, Ukraine, or Poland. They were growers and hunters but not at all technically or culturally advanced peoples. They were rural and driven southward by the need for food and the climatic benefits. They were decidedly basic peoples with a less sophisticated language and without military organization. They were also less politically organized and less interested in trade. Given who and what they were, they maneuvered around better-organized societies like the Magyars and found territorial gaps in various parts of the Balkans.

To the east, Russians and Kievian Rus (other Slavs) were confronting Turkic groups in and around Bulgaria and Belgrade. Both become part of the Slavic frontier. They benefit from being on the main route of the Crusaders from Western Europe to the lands of the eastern Mediterranean. Slavs turned out to be town builders; they accomplished this, however, by imitating the more advanced Venetian and Roman settlements. One of the Slavic tribes was the Pannonians whom the Romans managed as a colony around 700 A.D. They are not significantly different from other Slavs (though they are later distinguished by adopting Roman Catholicism). Croats are fond of suggesting that they were "independent" in the tenth century; upon careful scrutiny, however, the reality seems to be that a dynastic struggle left a temporary void during which one aspiring prince declared the colony independent, only to be swept aside by stronger forces in very short order. In 1102, Croatia joined Hungary and from that point on was linked with Austria and Europe for its development. In the history of Central and Southeast Europe, Croatia has been a middle-range player most often content with its supporting role in various empires.

Before long, all of the Balkan states were overshadowed by the emerging Venetian Empire, which took its place as the richest of empires from roughly 1200 to 1670. Built on commerce and its penchant for the sea, the Republic of Venice dominated the sea lanes for six centuries. It pursued a strategy that passed over opportunities to control land masses and instead focused all its energy and resources on building wealth by controlling key ports and trading posts. It is an empire, in retrospect, brilliantly conceived of "coasts, islands and isolated fortresses."[3] Its strategy was predicated on the notion that controlling land masses was difficult and costly, inviting conflict. By the 1400s, all of Dalmatia (literally the Dalmatian coast) was controlled by Venice. The interior lands beyond the coastal mountains (Bosnia, Hercegovina, Montenegro) were defaulted to the Ottoman Empire.

The Venetians were among the very first to refine politics by placing power in the hands of what we today call "technocrats." They contributed to modern politics in a host of ways. They recognized and built "incentive compatibility" into their political system. They formatted a grand jury, whistle-blowing, tax deductions, philanthropy, and a curious device for the protection of politicians called *in cognito*. The Venetians also curbed the power of the church in various ways and attempted to design into the system constraints on protest. They diluted mechanisms for representation by having the elected body play a very limited role in policymaking or policy-monitoring. Though these dimensions seem to tear in different directions, the Venetian political system enjoyed high levels of legitimacy and mass support for the institutional political design. One might speculate that there may be a subtle lesson for democratic politics today: Venice, the wealthiest state in its day, was able to achieve impressively high levels of public support without decentralizing power or embracing an explicitly democratic compact with its citizens. Perhaps wealth and the ripple effect of that wealth resulted in legitimacy for the political leadership in spite of the absence of many institutions that we often associate with nurturing legitimacy or democracy.

The Ottomans instituted a system embedded with some very positive features. Many could be particularly useful in the design of a political psychology that could and would support democratization today. The Ottoman Turks were a dominant force in the Balkans from 1281 to 1923. The overlap with Venetian power is considerable. Both were "superpowers" with what were then expansive empires. But the strategies could not have been more dissimilar, which may explain how they were able to coexist. The Ottomans controlled land, vast chunks often with sparse populations and little economic value. The Venetians, on the other hand, controlled only the tiny outposts that served their robust commercial interests. The geography of the Ottomans appears more impressive: Anatolia, the Middle East, North Africa, and much of Southeast Europe. Broadly speaking, Europeans felt threatened by the Ottoman Empire, and the immediate venue for this threat was the Balkans.

Politically, the Ottomans ruled in an elaborately decentralized pattern of indirect political control. The central feature of their system was the military hierarchy; political management for them was a tertiary focus. Their approach to the necessary political management of large numbers of markedly diverse peoples was ingenious and pivoted around finding local authorities to entrust. This technique is not adequately recognized for its effectiveness. Most histories report that virtually all Ottoman Turkish emperors married non-Turkish women. The resulting offspring had a new and mixed ethnic identity: Ottoman. Viziers consistently were drawn from indigenous groups and had widely varied backgrounds. The strain of diverse peoples led the Ottomans to a system characterized by high tolerance for alien cultures and religions (especially compared to regimes in the Christian West). Officially, all citizens under Ottoman rule enjoyed freedom of religion.

The Ottoman Empire was uncharacteristic of its time. It absorbed and integrated many cultures and, in so doing, captured rather than discarded the human capital in its territory. The Ottoman Empire was a refuge for Jews who were experiencing intolerance in Spain and other parts of Europe. None of these notions should be exaggerated. Problems persisted, but in the vein of recognizing and strategizing about such fundamental issues as tolerance and what today would be called "federalism," the Ottoman Empire was cutting-edge.

The Austro-Hungarian Empire also plays a major role in the convoluted history of Southeast Europe. In the twelfth century, the Hungarians opted to be managed (perhaps protected) by the Austrians. As history unfolds, the Austrians become the major competitor of the French for control of the Adriatic. The Austrians' initial role was as "protector" of Venice. Given that Venice declined to raise an army, it was vulnerable only from the land approach and its wealth bought a guarantee from Austria to ward off any foe. As the Ottomans threatened to conquer the Slavic and Hungarian people of the region, Hungarian and Croatian governments turned to Austria for organization and insulation.

In 1670 the Austrian government, by surreptitious maneuvering, sold out the Venetians and the French seized Venice. The French design was to control the coast by way of the former Venetian ports and islands. The Austrians sought the land that the Ottomans controlled by rolling them back through the interior of the Balkans. With French attention focused elsewhere, Austrian control was most extensive from 1797 to 1815 when Istria, Dalmatia, and Dubrovnik were all assets of the Hapsburgs. The Hapsburg Empire had its own refined management style structured around patron-client relationships. The various elements all seemed content as long as each had another "people" to lord over; that is, a client state of their own. In the Austro-Hungarian Empire, Croatia was a client state of Hungary but content because it had client states or territories in Bosnia and Hercegovina. As a loser in the Great War (World War I), Croatia was cobbled together with other Balkan peoples (Slavic and others) in the Kingdom of the South Slavs that in 1929 became Yugoslavia.

Though it is hardly the purpose here, careful and prudent analysis of Balkan history reveals a great deal from which descendants could take pride. Yet, generally, that is not how attitudes and images have developed. Beyond that, our Euro-dominant age has chosen to view the region as peripheral and troubling. All of this has resulted in some official proclamations and political edicts prescribing that the Balkans shall be called "Southeast Europe." And while the rationale may not be fair or tightly reasoned, the consequence is likely to be positive. So we shall go with the flow and use Southeast Europe as our rubric.

Southeast Europe and Beyond

This analysis will not include Greece or Turkey, on the premise that they did not share the socialist experience and, given their early admission to NATO, have clear features that set them apart from the primary focus here. Their process toward democratization had a different point of departure and a very different context: the cold war. Other factors complicate our choices. Slovenia has been afforded membership in the European Union. More recently, Romania and Bulgaria have been extended membership. Croatia is approaching a timetable for accession. Macedonia, Montenegro, and Bosnia are encouraged but limited in what they can expect from the EU. Serbia presents additional issues stemming both from its hostilities with NATO in the 1990s and the nature of the relationship between Serbia and Kosovo. Kosovo continues to search for a status in the international community generally. The ten political systems under consideration for this volume are Albania, Bosnia, Bulgaria, Croatia, Kosovo, Macedonia, Montenegro, Romania, Serbia, and Slovenia. Ten political systems in dramatically different stages of political and economic development. They share a regional geographic footprint and many historical experiences. They all face challenges today stemming from the effort to renovate political attitudes and chart a new course toward a more productive and satisfying future. They also share the reality that all this is happening under the intense scrutiny of powerful forces outside the region.

"Democracy"

The World Bank and many other sources often approach the concept of democracy by way of euphemisms, including "good governance," "capacity building," "voice," and "empowerment." A more useful and specific approach reflected in the May 2005 study by Daniel Kaufmann, Aart Kray, and Massimo Mastruzzi for the World Bank entitled *Governance Matters IV,* aggregates governance indicators for 209 countries.[4] Their indicators are (1) voice and accountability, (2) political instability and violence, (3) government effectiveness, (4) regulatory quality, (5) rule of law, and (6) control of corruption.

While not explicitly measuring "democracy," this study tilts toward an assumption that a democratic trajectory is the preferred course. Interestingly, the study finds "no trends, for better or worse, in global averages of governance." On closer scrutiny, these indicators (updated for 1996–2004) draw their analysis away from the focus of this volume. For example, while voice and accountability are central to the plan for this volume, the World Bank study suggests that by "voice and accountability" it is "measuring political, civil and human rights." Similarly, a mutual concern for the "control of corruption" takes the two approaches far apart. The World Bank study purports to examine the "control of corruption" by measuring "the business elite's perception of the exercise of public power for private gain including both petty and grand corruption and state capture." This analysis will examine "corruption" as a negative indicator of a commitment to restraint and constraint among all elites. Another example of contrast with the World Bank's study is found in its use of what might be called "corporate" or macroeconomic lenses. The study itself acknowledges the significant difficulties associated with measuring governance in general and perceptions-based measures in particular. "Institutional quality" is especially elusive. The authors of the World Bank study refer to their indicators as "blunt instruments for specific policy assessment at the country level." Nonetheless, the study is instructive and valuable given its priorities and limitations.

The International Institute for Democracy and Electoral Assistance (IDEA) offers still more insight. It posits that "democracy is a contested concept."[5] This truism is compelling. Nonetheless, an effort is made to suggest that democracy is "a system of political governance whose decision-making power is subject to the controlling influence of citizens who are considered political equals. A democratic system is inclusive, participatory, representative, accountable, transparent and responsive to citizens' aspirations and expectations."[6] These values of democracy are realized by degree and are observable through political institutions and practices: "Democracy is not a linear process that moves from an authoritarian to a democratic regime."[7] In real-life settings, this process appears in fits and starts and is extraordinarily complex. At best, it reflects uneven textures between rhetoric and practice and among policies and procedures. IDEA argues that "assessment of democratic progress" actually becomes an "important part of defining and building" democracy. The institute shares the objective of this volume in assessing the condition of democracy. In contrast, it has tested its methodology in eight countries around the world. It also emphasizes attitudes and opinions by leaning on the global barometers network of surveys. Finally, it underscores the necessity for local governance. It argues that only decentralized governance can set locally specific development goals, sustain participatory decision-making, and preserve accountable management systems. IDEA suggests that such local dynamics "deepen commitment" to democracy and increase legitimacy.[8]

IDEA's work has contributed significantly to the state of our understanding. In its many publications, it has advanced the methodology, data, and clarity of the study of real-world democratic development.[9] They acknowledge that "democratization is NOT a result of automatic social processes but rather a product of human agency."[10] Their emphasis is set in the notion that *democracy must be "grounded" in local ownership of the political agenda and must be formulated by those who live in the political system and who are experiencing the transition.* This notion is much more than a passing reminder that democracy can identify many alternative "destinations." Experiences of other systems can contribute by "catalyzing the dialogue" about democracy building.

A region-specific focus at IDEA resulted in the 2002 program "South Eastern Europe: New Means for Regional Analysis." This program was a joint venture with the South Eastern Europe Democracy Support network. Its objective was to use local think tanks to perform surveys and interviews to establish "what democracy actually delivers to people." Transparently, it "sought to facilitate and promote democratic reform." As such it must be understood that it cast itself as advocate, as much as analyst. The series of country-based studies parallel the ten countries examined in this volume. Over a two-year period, the IDEA project interviewed 220 politicians, 10,000 other persons, and utilized 40 focus groups to decipher patterns of "hopes, expectations, challenges and concerns on the public agenda." Many of their findings will be shared in chapter 3.

The chapters that follow are organized around six elements that would indicate strong democratic direction in political development, if found in a political system. The reasoning inherent in these six elements is shared below. The mechanics and manifestations of each may be open for debate, but the central conditions that each represents are drawn from mainstream democratic thought. These elements are tolerance, obligation, voice, constraint, transparency, and legitimacy.

Tolerance is a broad political value that triggers the behaviors essential to create and sustain democracy. But its necessity goes well beyond that. Capitalism requires tolerance in the form of appreciation for the intrinsic value of competition. The education system that is required in a democratic setting can only be premised on intellectual tolerance; that is, an environment where a full range of ideas find expression. Democracy does not compel us to like, value, or promote competing ideas, groups, leaders, firms, or products. It demands that we tolerate them: in essence, to agree in advance to coexist with such things to which others attach value. In this crucial sense, tolerance is the basis for inclusion, which, in turn, can reduce the sense of victimization—or in more positive terms, can induce a minimum level of comfort among the governed.

Obligation is the idea that government is mandated to seek out and mirror public sentiment, and to pursue publicly defined interests, albeit selectively and on its own schedule. This involves the structures that are built into the political architecture of the system. Legislatures, interest groups, and editorials may serve as examples. It also requires leadership behavior that frames, reinforces, and institutionalizes the mandate. In a democracy, this is not an option. Obligation provides focus for those governing and compels them to appreciate the ruminations of the masses.

Voice is an element that represents potential power as much as manifest power in a political system. The channels need to be open, accessible, and understood by the general public, even though they may be used intermittently. In political systems, voice is the capacity to send a signal, the confidence that it will be heard, and the potential that it will resonate between elites and masses. Democracies create public space for coalescing and manifesting voice. Perception of this commitment in the minds of both rulers and those ruled is key.

Constraint is the notion that those in power understand and accept that they are constrained to curb their impulses to exercise authority. This notion involves behavior that conforms to system mandates and the appreciation for the need to impose on oneself added boundaries to promote the balance between individual and collective interests in the society. Political authorities are expected to be both constrained and restrained in their conduct.

Transparency is a rather straightforward idea. If democracy compels the governed to have opinions and play some role in interacting with those in power, the governed must be able to see whose authority is being exercised and when. Given that this openness does not happen naturally in bureaucracies, the system must design windows that can shed light on operations, decisions, and administration when the public or its agents choose to scrutinize the authorities. Commitment to procedures that make this possible and productive is central to democratic processes.

Legitimacy is the vision that the governed have of those in authority. As such, it may reflect many of the assessments made of the other five dimensions. The public is the singular source of legitimacy: specifically, the sense that those in power achieved that authority by proper and established (prescribed) means. Legitimacy may be measured periodically but is, in fact, a persistent and fluid factor in the texture of any political system. One role remains crucial for the public: they have the responsibility to accept or reject the path to power. With this established, it is predictable that they will also evaluate the leadership.

The six elements outlined here are broad conditions that will be nurtured if a political system is to set its course toward democracy. Each can be observed evolving in a society by gauging a number of empirical features of a system's architecture and behavior. We shall want to be cautious about rhetoric and labeling; these devices are often used to create illusions about actual progress toward democracy. It is perhaps most useful to imagine each of the six elements as a continuum on which we shall place our ten countries as we develop this analysis.

Foundations in the Literature

No doubt stimulated by the effort to export "democracy" or its likeness to other parts of the world, the academic literature has become rich with recent studies that wrestle with democratic development. *Democracy Challenged: The Rise of Semi-Authoritarianism* (Washington, D.C.: Carnegie Endowment for International Peace, 2003) by Marina Ottaway stands out among these. The clarity of Ottaway's analysis and her comparative examples illuminate the full range of problems that beset transitioning political systems. One of her featured examples is Croatia under Tudjman. Another very useful and heuristic volume is Charles F. Andrain and James T. Smith's *Political Democracy, Trust, and Social Justice* (Boston: Northeastern University Press, 2006). It uses a broader comparative approach to examine textures of thinking in crystallizing democracies and is especially valuable to this analysis both in its examination of attitudes surrounding personal versus political life (see their chapter 5) and in its conclusion which, in the context of Southeast Europe, reminds one of the nationalism and autonomy tensions. Bulgaria is one of the fifteen states compared in their volume.

Noam Chomsky's *Failed States: The Abuse of Power and the Assault on Democracy* (New York: Metropolitan Books, 2006) contributes to our understanding of how crucial it is to be "measured" in our approach to democratic development. It steels any analysis against the inclination to neglect blemishes or to become cavalier about the depth of patterns (scars) that must be overcome to support democracy. John E. Mueller's *Capitalism Democracy and Ralph's Pretty Good Grocery* (Princeton, N.J.: Princeton University Press, 1999), using a radically different framework, builds to a similar central theme: democracy is an imperfect but often idealized system that at best can be "pretty good" even in optimal circumstances. It can never be so egalitarian nor so participatory as its proponents claim.

Aiding Democracy Abroad: The Learning Curve (Washington, D.C.: Carnegie Endowment for International Peace, 1999) by Thomas Carothers reveals how polarized most analyses have become as they examine transitions toward democracy. He sees the debates as largely unhealthy: swinging wildly from "extreme skepticism" to unrealistic and uncritical boosterism. Carothers examines a range of elements in the "democracy template" and discusses meaningfully how external assistance might be improved. In this sense, his book shares some synergy with this volume: prescriptions are made here not for the external actors but rather for the systems themselves and for their leadership.

Ronald Inglehart and Christian Welzel's *Modernization, Cultural Change and Democracy* (New York: Cambridge University Press, 2005) is framed around the notion that economic development and cultural maturation must serve as the basis (value basis) for the development of democracy. In the context of Southeast Europe, that study serves as a critical reminder not only of the values that are requisite but also of the time dimension required to promote and solidify democracy in the region. With time allowed for such evolution, the authors are rather optimistic about the path toward democracy. Even more vulnerable to the criticism that it is tilted to optimism is *Consolidating the Third Wave Democracies* (Baltimore: Johns Hopkins University Press, 1997), edited by Larry Diamond. The "wave" is said to have "brought down" authoritarian regimes; while "still fragile," democracies are continuing to consolidate. While the volume does inventory the challenges faced, it is prone to see these as likely to be met. Lisa Anderson's *Transitions to Democracy* (New York: Columbia University Press, 1999) benefits from the single author's logic but also is inclined to find the path of transitioning systems clearly marked toward "democracy." Of course, no review of the current literature on democracy would be possible without highlighting the major reference work on the subject, *The Democracy Sourcebook* (Cambridge, Mass.: MIT Press, 2003) by Robert Dahl, Ian Shapiro, and Josntonio Cheibub. Of special importance for this analysis is its contribution to defining democracy and the effort to illuminate the "pre-conditions" for democracy.

There remain a few recent studies of democratization in the region that warrant highlighting. Attila Agh's *Emerging Democracies in East Central Europe and the Balkans* (Northampton, Mass.: E. Elgar, 1998) is an analysis in the area studies genre that provides rich detail, especially on states that are often dismissed as minor actors. It advances our sense of the process of democratization in the region but concludes before the events of the late 1990s. Also of limited value is the Centre for Liberal Strategies' *The Inflexibility Trap: Frustrated Societies, Weak States and Democracy* (Sofia, Bulgaria: Data Agency, 2003), a partial analysis with some methodological vulnerability but nonetheless useful as background. Also taking a rather narrow angle on the region but building on detailed country studies is *Endgame in the Balkans: Regime Change European Style* (Washington, D.C.: Brookings Institution Press, 2006) by Elizabeth Pond. A thoughtful work is *Challenges to New Democracies in the Balkans* (Belgrade: Association of Fulbright Alumni of Serbia and Montenegro, 2004), edited by Slobodan G. Markovich, Eric Beckett Weaver, and Vukasin Pavlovic. It provides useful first-person insight into some transitional issues.

Sabrina P. Ramet's *Balkan Babel* (4th ed.; Boulder, Colo.: Westview, 2002) is an outstanding vision of the disintegration of Yugoslavia. With clear detail, it charts the events and consequences of the period through the demise of Milošević. It does not offer prescriptions for the future development of the political system as I shall in this volume. Two other volumes contribute to the sound regional literature: *Europe Undivided: Democracy, Leverage, and Integration after Communism* (New York: Oxford University Press, 2005), by

Milada Anna Vachudovaia; and *Capitalism and Democracy in Central and Eastern Europe: Assessing the Legacy of Communist Rule* (New York: Cambridge University Press, 2003), edited by Grzegorz Ekiert and Stephen E. Hanson. Both are strong descriptive analyses of thrusts toward institutionalizing democratic structures in the postcommunist states. The first focuses more on the EU's impact, the latter on internal structural reforms.

None of these studies reach far into this century and none choose to be prescriptive in any detail. All seem comfortable presuming the wisdom of a liberal, democratic course for these postcommunist transitioning systems. Thus I have the courage to place my volume alongside those studies. Clearly, any analysis of the sort offered here is indebted to the scholarly work that preceded it.

Transition from Communism

It is necessary at this point to suggest a broader framework that will enable us to locate the various elements that will be discussed. Simply stated, to emerge as democratic political systems, weather the storms associated with transition from a nondemocratic system, and survive the long-term strains of maintaining a democratic political environment, a political system must acquire or establish three things:

1. A generic *value system* shared by the bulk of the governed—ideas and expectations that enable the leaders to communicate with, and anticipate the behavior of, the publics they are attempting to lead.
2. *Political machinery*—structures or mechanisms institutionalized to the point that they are recognized and can produce the outcomes (policies) that the leadership is aiming toward.
3. *Leadership*—a cadre of persons able to pursue goals by making rational policy choices, accounting for costs, payoffs, and consequences.

A bit more explanation is required. Values are the platform for both attitudes and behavior. Casual political rhetoric in democracies often leaves one with the impression that everyone in society "does their own thing" or can go in whatever direction they wish. Political systems wishing to become democratic are essentially saying that they wish to take the society where the masses themselves say they want to go. The tough question becomes, what happens in societies in which both government and governed are inexperienced with democratic relationships to the point that the public comes to believe that each person in society really *can* set his or her own agenda (or destination) for government? This conception is evident in Southeast Europe. Imagine a new leader genuinely committed to taking the society where it wants to go. He or she asks the public to point toward that destination, and what follows is the unpatterned response of a "free" public. Everyone points in a different direction: up or down, right or left, forward or back. How can the leader take the system in all those directions at once? It is not possible. The system then has the unenviable choice of either abandoning the notion that it will take the masses where they want to go, or pretending that there is a consensus about direction coming from the masses. The point is basic but important. Functioning democratic systems require a consensus about direction, about destination, even if broad or vague. Established democracies have this. Transitional systems typically do not. Constructing that consensus is the first, critical task for postcommunist systems.

If a consensus emerges from the public about where they want government to take them, the next task is the construction of a vehicle that the public can board for the journey toward the destination. Thus we shift attention to the political machinery and the political architecture for that machinery. Imagine this machinery as the bus that could move a large mass of people toward a common goal. Naturally, reaching the destination is less critical than making progress along the path toward it. One pondering this analogy might ask: Why is it necessary to have a bus? Can't folks in a society walk toward their destination and implicitly set their own individual pace? Of course they can, and when one examines many of the political systems in our world, it often looks as if that is what is happening. But the twenty-first century is a keenly global, competitive, and transparent era, in which many societies have already embarked on their own journeys, using political machinery that gets them along their paths more quickly and effectively. People in one society are likely to be displeased with their progress, just as one walking along the side of the road is displeased when a bus zips past toward a similar destination. What all this means for our political look at Southeast European systems is that we must be careful to examine how assembled and functional the institutional parts of the political and economic system are. "Transition" implies the bus is only partially assembled.

Completing the metaphor, the leadership of a society functions like the driver of the bus. The driver will certainly play a major role in defining the speed, path, and maneuvering essential to move the society toward its goals or destination. The skills of the driver must not be presumed. Transitional systems are driving along new paths, slick, untested, and fraught with hazards and unanticipated detours. As irony would have it, "drivers" in established democracies need fewer skills because institutional ruts in the road more clearly guide their journey and behavior. Furthermore, they evolve in systems that teach and test their driving skills before they take on driving the "bus." Transitional systems have no such advantages. Their paths are without many institutional patterns or grooves, and most of the leaders find themselves in positions of great authority without previous experience—certainly without experience in a democratic context.

The Former System in Brief

Communism advocated a goal of economic equality, or "economic democracy," which in practical terms meant a leveling of the society economically. These values, coupled with the government's control of prices and distribution, created a belief that many goods and services should be guaranteed by government. Functionally, this was the value consensus for that system. There was also an elaborate political machinery. The single Communist Party was designed and refined over time to perform one primary function: to maintain its exclusive hold on power. If the machine's effectiveness were judged *only* in those terms, it functioned well until Mikhail Gorbachev began tinkering with the machine. In comparative terms, the political machinery of the communist system was as extensive, bureaucratized, and penetrating as any in the twentieth century. Setting aside for the moment what one may think about a system designed to keep itself in power, there can be little doubt that both a broad value system and a developed political machine existed in communist systems.

It is far less clear that the old system generated a minimum level of leadership that could direct and manage those societies. The recruitment system, the inadequate education system (in terms of policy-relevant studies), the propensity to quash issue-oriented debate, the minimal relationship between rulers and ruled, and the very vertical nature of the political system combined to ensure mediocre leadership. The leadership in Southeast Europe was generally detached, noninnovative, and passive. It failed to acknowledge that political systems must adapt to inevitably changing circumstances and environments. It ultimately revealed itself incapable of calculating the costs, payoffs, and consequences of major policy decisions. There were a few exceptions to this pattern, notably in socialist Yugoslavia (discussed further on in this volume). But generally, the pattern of politics produced leadership that was the weakest link in the political system. It was characteristically inept, narrow in its thinking, and timid. It committed more energy to maintaining illusions than to solving problems. The political landscape in the 1980s was dominated by uncertainty and unsolidified change.

Value Consensus: Principal Agents

Of central concern is who is contributing to the formation of a value consensus in these relatively new transitional political systems. Leaders play some role. Television, the Internet, and the European Union all have key roles in bringing a common future into sharper focus for the public in these transitional societies. Beyond them are international agencies, the International Monetary Fund and the World Bank that have as their explicit task guiding societies toward a prepackaged model or destination. Although there is significant debate about the wisdom of this or that destination, the only point offered here is that political development in these societies, at this stage, requires that there be a destination defined by a broad and general consensus. Some political theorists call this a "common story" or "narrative," but whatever it is called, political societies in the twenty-first century will have great difficulty *drifting* toward democracy.

Two other agents play roles with varying levels of effectiveness: religion and education. Education is a powerful element in the dialogue. The education infrastructure in Bosnia, for example, was so thoroughly destroyed or compromised by the violence of the 1990s that it is impossible to recognize it as an actor in the effort to create a consensus. A study generated by the Times Higher Education Supplement (November 5, 2004) ranked the world's two hundred "top" universities; not one Southeast European university made the list. Religion is discussed in a number of the chapters that follow.

The absence of a consensus in Southeast Europe in the early 1990s was a function of the process by which communism ended. Large numbers of persons and groups in communist countries (including some Communist Party members) concluded that the communist regimes were not meeting the minimum obligations that *they* had laid out. In a nutshell, broad and diverse movements began to grow quickly in Central and Southeast Europe that shared a vision of what people were against. Solidarity (Poland), the Civic Forum (Czechoslovakia), the Democratic Forum (Hungary), Yeltsin's ad hoc effort to save Gorbachev (USSR, August 1991), and the violent spasm that brought down the Ceauşescu regime in Romania were all high-visibility movements reflecting a strong sense of what was *not* wanted. Each of these movements, however, disintegrated when the time came to establish what the public *did* want. The point is that a consensus did not grow out of these movements. The task of establishing one fell on the subsequent governments. The difficulty was apparent, and some still are unable to frame a constructive consensus.

Political Architecture

The most significant development that accelerated the search for common values was the emergence of the European Union. By 1992, just as communism was disintegrating in the region, Western Europe was raising its level of integration from the European "Community" to the European "Union." In essence, the integration made the relationships in the region more binding and involved some sacrifice of political sovereignty by member states. As political systems in the postcommunist region began foundering, the European Union provided for these countries an elaborated set of societal goals and an organizational destination best captured in the EU's requisites for formal membership. It should be added that these conditions are negotiable and flexible given sundry interpretations and situations:

- A stable system of democratic government
- Institutions that ensure the rule of law and respect for human rights
- A functioning and competitive market economy
- An administration capable of implementing EU laws and policies

These conditions should be understood as setting the destination for aspiring member societies—past, present, and future. The general pattern of European integration has become a path of choice for most Southeast European systems precisely because it addressed the challenges of establishing a value consensus (destination) and because it brings with it defined architecture for institutional development and the funds to implement it. The path that has emerged prescribes that a country first connect with NATO, and then use that legitimacy as a platform for EU membership. It has become apparent that the dialogue and behavior associated with NATO membership moves the broader integration along expeditiously. Bulgaria and Romania are the best regional examples of this, but in Central Europe, Poland, the Czech Republic, Slovakia, Hungary, and the Baltic States all followed this path. Croatia, Macedonia, Albania, and Montenegro have also engaged in negotiations to establish a firm path toward NATO membership (target date 2008). Those discussions often center not on military requisites but rather on elements of democracy and broad institutional development, thus creating a linear path to EU membership. The focus on corruption, media, elections, law, and other elements are the very ones examined in the pages that follow.

Effective Leadership

New leadership in Southeast Europe is a requisite for political development. To reiterate, communist leadership was timid, poorly skilled in policymaking and without incentive to pursue systemic goals. The range of leadership qualities found in Southeast Europe today is vast. The range of commitment to real democratic development is also significant. Political careers in the new political environment are especially unstable. The new political systems have managed to identify a small number of bright, polished, and articulate leaders whose personal dedication to leadership, as they see it, is impressive. Leaders as a general rule fall into one of three categories. The first is what can be usefully called "born-again democrats." They were leaders in the former communist era. They claimed to have "seen the light" (that is, the error of their ways in the old system) and are prepared to promote the new values and institutions in the transition. In essence, they claim to be politically reborn and are committed to the new politics, including the efficacy of elections and pluralism. Most have struggled. They discovered that they were usually unprepared to deal with the criticism, compromise, and transparency characteristic in the new environment. Milošević (Serbia), Tudjman (Croatia), Iliescu (Romania), and Berisha (Albania) nonetheless persisted in power and are examples of the born-agains who demonstrated the weaknesses outlined. Still other born-agains managed to renovate their thinking and have established more credibility in their approach to the new political environment. These include Zhelev (Bulgaria), Kučan (Slovenia), and Mesić (Croatia). These persons characteristically have articulated their ideological skepticism with the old system, arguing that they needed to work in the old system to change it.

The second group is "rookies." They argue that their inexperience with political leadership under the old regime is an asset. They claim that any relationship with the old system is contaminating and that as "virgin" politicians they are untainted. This approach apparently had initial appeal. In time, the public began to recognize that inexperience was not an asset, especially in political situations that demanded sophisticated solutions to difficult problems compounded by limited resources.

The last group is "imports." Often they are established and accomplished in professions other than politics in a country to which they or their families migrated. The United States, Canada, France, Britain and Italy—all contributed some of these want-to-be politicians. One Serbian prime minister, Milan Panić, was a California businessman. Boris Mikšić, a Minnesota chemical company CEO, ran for president of Croatia, finishing third. Imported (and in some cases *re*imported) professionals were assumed to know about effective leadership because they had led companies successfully or simply because they had lived in the kind of political system that their new Southeast European state was trying to create. All such "imports" have struggled in their pursuit of political power, although the stories differ with each example.

Confidence and Leadership

Born-agains understood best the system from which society was distancing itself. In cases where their personal political transformation was incomplete, they hampered reforms. They also found that they were largely unprepared for the rigors of democratic and pluralistic politics. The public also recognized quickly that rookies were ill-equipped to appreciate the complexity of what they were trying to do. The learning curve for many was steep, and the impact on both regimes and society was costly. Imports, by and large, were revealed to be out of touch and suffered from some of the same ills as rookies.

Southeast European leadership echelons reveal a clear generational gap. The born-agains are older and are increasingly marginalized or disappearing altogether with the passage of time. Rookies, on the other hand, have become more assertive and more confident. Hope lies in the generation of new but not inexperienced leaders who are developing backgrounds colored in with education, international exposure, and an awareness of the sophistication needed to be effective. Youthful confidence is giving way to measured clarity of purpose. Whatever one might think of the ideological texture of the evolving, middle-aged leadership in Southeast Europe, it is clear that these are the people in whom power will be vested. Their education tells them that the EU and Europe is the safest framework for their society's development. They will try, with varying degrees of success, to convince their respective publics.

The major difference between the leadership dilemma of the first years of transition and today is the emergence of leaders with a sound basis for their confidence. They can and do use the external advice and guidance they get. They measure it against a growing pool of internal advisers and experts. Perhaps more important, many of them remain committed to a political process involving public input, turnover, transparency, and compromise. These dynamics will be examined in the chapters that follow. To frame the general situation in terms of the analogy, most leaders in Southeast Europe are still far from experienced "drivers," but they understand better than ever before that driving a bus is tough, that it demands all of their focus, and that turning the task over to another driver at some point is normal and necessary.

We proceed then with a broad framework that will enable us to place our analysis on the specific six dimensions.

Chapter 2

Tolerance

Democracy is a system of government which provides tentative
and tolerable solutions to insoluble problems.

A key value that raises concern about democratic development in Southeast
Europe is the centrality of tolerance to democracy. The perspective offered
here suggests that tolerance is the absolute cornerstone of a functioning democratic and capitalist system. Tolerance is the conceptual platform that enables
the debate requisite to compromise. It is the glue that holds together societies
that are just beginning to work through issues that involve heterogeneity and
political debate. Most Southeast European societies have very little experience
with tolerance.

Hallmark periods of power in the region have been associated with intolerance and exploitation for most of the twentieth century (many would argue,
well beyond that). Most recently, the communist period was insensitive to the
systemic costs associated with stifling human initiative and divergent voices.
Conformity and pattern were high values. One residual perception growing out
of the communist experience is the notion that a single ideology is the magical,
correct one and that the accommodation of others is unproductive and, at worst,
sabotage. From a superficial perspective, many believe that greatness comes
with strength and strength is demonstrated by centralized, authoritarian management. By this line of reasoning, tolerance is weakness and or uncertainty.
The region's politics has been characterized by aspiring authoritarian figures
and movements that for the most part had only brief political life cycles.
Romania, Serbia, Croatia, Bulgaria, Macedonia, and Albania have all had patterns of actively intolerant political regimes. Perhaps most poignant is the recent pattern of intolerance evident in nearly every aspect of politics in Bosnia.

Capitalism

It may be a bit unorthodox to see tolerance as the core feature of market-
competitive capitalism. Nonetheless, it is one of the essential values around

which the economic system and its incumbent behaviors are manifest. Without the tolerance of competing forces in the economy—domestic or international—capitalism could not exist nor evolve. If the modal value among businesses were predatory, the pluralistic marketplace would not long survive. Remembering that for many in Southeast Europe these are new lessons and behaviors, it is possible to observe the frictions that come with the economic and political transition.

Europe's economists and prominent political leaders have offered a number of prescriptions to accelerate and ensure positive economic change in the region. Among them is a proposal for a free trade zone. It is in some sense a litmus test by which one can gauge the measure of residual intolerance versus the openness to reengineering that would signal growing tolerance. In practical terms, it signals a population's willingness to embrace products from neighboring states or other internal regions.

One specific proposal of this sort would have Croatia, Serbia, Montenegro, Bosnia, Macedonia and Albania operating under the open trade system in 2007. The EU leadership clearly sees this system as ameliorating much of the economic dislocation created by the breakup of Yugoslavia. It might also dilute some of the ethnic tensions that persist. The idea has been confronted by the same political resistance to any proposals that appear to turn the clock back to a united Yugoslavia, even if only on a practical economic basis. Nonetheless, the idea may be too much to resist, given the forthright way the EU is prepared to broker it as a step toward membership. It will certainly be a test of tolerance, a gauge of the balance between emotion and pragmatism.

The Croatian public, in early 2006, were against this proposal by a 2:1 margin with 30 percent expressing no opinion.[1] The Croatia government is delicately maneuvering by proposing the expansion of the Central European Free Trade Association, a more palatable solution from its perspective. The hope is that this expansion will elicit a different perception and avoid the political baggage that the EU plan does. Once an EU member, Croatia would find it useful to extend membership to those states that are a part of the EU proposal.

Ivica Račan, a former prime minister and leader of the Social Democrats, suggested that such fears of a "new Yugoslavia" gobbling up Croatia play on the anxieties of the poorly informed. The European Commission emphasizes that the goal is to create a single market big enough to entice greater foreign investment and strengthen the region's competitive position. The population of the proposed zone would be twenty-four million. In 2005, overall trade between the western Balkan states (Croatia, Serbia, Bosnia, Montenegro, Macedonia, Albania) rose by 50 percent. Croatia's gross national product per capita is €6,220, more than three times the regional average of €2,000. In Bosnia it is a meager €1,730. Most economists believe that the free trade zone would speed the entire region's progress toward EU integration with significant implications for democratic processes and behaviors.

The essence of this example is simply to demonstrate that from a functional and pragmatic perspective, the idea of economic flows across borders is sound. Historical memory and prejudice, however, may result in policies that damage the trajectory of a society and its economy. To recognize tolerance in its economic manifestation as the element of competition is crucial to understanding why tolerance is a cornerstone value if democracy is to be developed.

Religious Pluralism

We are quite naturally drawn to the religious realm when assessing tolerance in a society. Signals from Serbia and elsewhere have set a skeptical tone. In early 2006, leadership in Serbia's powerful Orthodox Church (Patriarch Pavle in Vojvodina) complained of harassment and demanded action to prevent attacks on Serbian Orthodox churches, facilities, clergy, and believers. He wanted a political statement from the government that hate speech against the church (Serbian Orthodox) was intolerable. Revealing how intertwined and messy such issues can be, the actual statements that triggered the demand involved regional politicians who have taken antinationalist positions. The notion that the Serbian Orthodox Church is a victim is rather problematic, given that it has often benefited from preferential treatment in Serbia.

A prominent Serbian journalist with B92 (a very popular radio station), Mirolsav Zadrenko, observed, "Far from being mistreated or sidelined, the Serbian Orthodox Church (SPC) is widely seen as the country's most influential religious organization by far. It often supported Serbian combatants in the conflicts that raged over the former Yugoslavia in the Nineties, while some clergy became notorious for involvement with extremist paramilitaries."[2]

The Center for Development of Civil Society is a Serbian civil rights organization that has addressed this and other sensitive issues: "The Serbian church is "unaccustomed to any criticism at all." "Just as we [in civil society] must get used to such public statements, the SPC should accustom itself to criticism." "Serbia is becoming a state of one confession only." "At the time when the Bajrakli mosque [attacked by hooligans in Belgrade in retaliation for violence against Kosovo Serbs in March 2004] has not yet been fully reconstructed, and the same goes for the mosque in Nis, the government proves . . . that it only cares about one religious community."[3] The Independent Journalists' Association of Vojvodina called on the authorities finally to adopt a bill on religious freedom that would ban all forms of religious discrimination. Political systems throughout the region have been unable to muster a commitment to tolerate all religious groups. Characteristically, each religious hierarchy presses for tolerance of its own practice but fails to endorse the tolerance of all others.

Another contemporary example is the recent case in Macedonia. Leading churchmen in Macedonia say documentation from the Serbian Ministry of Religion confirms that Belgrade is financing a parallel Orthodox church in Macedonia.[4] The example speaks to the intolerant posturing of both Serbia and Macedonia. It also underlines the apparently odd reality that various Orthodox churches are genuinely intolerant of one another. The Macedonian Orthodox Church (MPC), revealed a formal document in March 2006 that seems to prove that Serbia's government is the real force behind the parallel church created and led by a renegade Macedonian cleric. Serbia's minister of religion, Milan Radulovic, confirmed the authenticity of the document. He said money was sent to the Ohrid archdiocese with the approval of Serbian Prime Minister Vojislav Koštunica. Yet, the government in Belgrade says it has nothing to apologize for. Serbian law allows for "the provision of support and assistance for the protection of the ecclesiastical cultural heritage outside the borders of the Serbia-Montenegro State Union." It added that this provision also legitimizes "the advancement of the religious aspect of national identity beyond the borders of the State Union [Serbia and Montenegro]."

Such religious conflicts are complex and impenetrable to outsiders, who often find the Macedonian Orthodox Church's privileged relations to the state idiosyncratic and inconsistent with a secular, pluralistic society. The current Macedonian government shows no sign of relaxing support for the MPC's demands to retain a monopoly on the profession of Orthodox Christianity in Macedonia. Macedonian law outlaws two religious communities holding the same confession. "We have only one institutionally recognized Orthodox Church in Macedonia," espoused Cane Mojanovski, head of the government commission for relations with religious communities. The Macedonian government position is that Serbia and the Serbian Orthodox Church are trying to "pull up the roots of Macedonia's national identity." Macedonian Bishop Timotej claims, "It is obvious the Serbian church does not care about creating normal relations but instead wants to destroy and torment the whole nation, state and church."[5]

While Macedonian clerics triumphantly presented the controversial document to EU and U.S. ambassadors in Skopje, Macedonia's Foreign Ministry sent an ironic protest to Belgrade, reminding it "of the necessity to respect the principle of state non-interference in church matters." This statement is ironic indeed, given the Macedonian government's intense engagement with managing the religious environment in Macedonia. Mirko Djordjević, a religious expert in Belgrade, conceded the Macedonian point. "Any relationship between the Belgrade political leadership and that organisation [the Ohrid archdiocese] from the Macedonian perspective, is a relationship with an illegal organization, which complicates things enormously."

The real threat to democratization appears to be the policy that would provide and support a single religious organization with a dominant position. This support could readily nudge any political system in the region toward the creation of a fundamentalist state.[6]

Competitive Media

The working environment for journalists and the public's ability to be informed are two of the dimensions that illuminate a system design that reinforces tolerance. A competitive media (sometimes called an "open" media) requires collaboration among government, the fourth estate, and the active public. It is not an easily achieved synergy. It does not lend itself to a standard formula. Even in a region with much common heritage, it appears that each political system creates its own nuanced media landscape.

The Macedonian case is instructive.[7] Manipulation by either government, business interests (private media owners), or a foreign government is a persistent threat. In 2006 the public in Macedonia became aware of a group of journalists who worked for a public relations firm that was ultimately responsible to government ministers. This conflict of interest exposed one of the relationships that undermines the integrity of an independent media. Working journalists clandestinely wrote speeches for ruling Social Democrat ministers and even colluded with officials to choreograph press conferences. Sloppy standards and malleable ethics characterize the media landscape in most of the region.

An opinion poll conducted at the beginning of 2006 said more than 70 percent of those interviewed no longer trusted the media. The Association of Journalists reports, "Macedonia breaks records in the region for the number of media outlets per capita, with 48 television stations, over 160 radio stations, and nine daily and eight weekly newspapers in a population of 2.1 million. But this abundance does not bring quality." Zoran Ivanov, director of the state-owned Macedonian Information Agency is among those who have blamed the ownership structure for declining standards. Deregulation has erased prohibitions that barred politicians from owning media. One result is that political parties now own, or are closely linked to, three of the five private television stations licensed to broadcast over Macedonia's entire territory.

In autumn 2006, Macedonia adopted a new freedom of information act. The journalist's plight in the region is difficult and may explain some of the "malleable ethics." What some call a climate of corruption may be encouraged by the reality that 75 percent of the thousand journalists in Macedonia do not receive regular salaries; even when paid, they receive minimal compensation. No effort to represent the measure to which tolerance is solidifying in a system could neglect the informational landscape of the society and the media's role in it. Examples abound of situations that detract from the appearance that broad and diverse media messages are the priority.

Multiparty Systems

One tangible indicator of tolerance manifesting itself in a political system is a functioning multiparty political system. The practical dynamic of political dialogue, negotiation, coalition formation, and maintenance at an intermediate political level in society establishes a pattern of cooperative as well as competitive behavior. Competitive, that is, within the bounds of the systemic rules. If the political parties are designed around other than ethnic (nationalistic) interests, the support for tolerance is more meaningful. Similarly, if the parties coalesce around issues rather than individual candidates, the contribution to an evolving democratic system is more enduring. Multiple issue-centric political parties can contribute to steadiness and pattern in the political environment generally.

Political party systems have evolved in these transitional states in an unguided fashion. Some cues from other, more established European systems are evident but almost every state has its own distinguishable pattern. The healthiest seem to have between four and eight parties that actively participate in legislatures by having reached whatever threshold is prescribed. The Slovene example is one that has worked effectively, with eight of its parties making the 4 percent vote total requirement. The labels and platforms represent broad sectors of the ideological spectrum for the most popular parties (Liberal Democrats, Social Democrats, Slovenian People's Party, and the Christian Democrats. The "United List" Party is the resurrected Communist Party. The Slovene system also has a number of parties that make narrower appeals to voters including the Democratic Party of Retired People, Slovenian Nationalist Party, and the Slovenian Youth Party. As the system develops, it is reasonable to expect some of these smaller parties will grow either into interest groups with the advantage of dialoguing with all controlling parties (or coalitions) or melding into the more popular parties and maintaining a caucus status within those. In terms of tolerance, the spectrum appears reasonably well reflected in the array of parties. Few rules exist that constrain party activity. The notable exceptions are rules on accounting for funds and assets and the threshold itself, which discriminates against sliver elements in the electorate.

Croatia also seems to be moving in a positive, tolerant direction, though with more ground to cover compared to Slovenia. It currently has seventeen parties in the legislature with a total number of 110 registered political parties. This number certainly covers the ideological landscape but also indicates that there is a good deal of dialogue and compromise that has yet to take place before a patterned party system stabilizes. The Croatian Democratic Party (Christian Democratic Union) remains a powerful force while the Democratic Center Party, Croatian People's Party, the Croatian Peasant Party and the Socialist Liberals make some broad appeals. Most of the other parties are focused narrowly, including the Party of Rights, the Independent Democratic Serbia Party, the Party of Pensioners, the Istrian Democratic Alliance, and the Social Democrats. Nearly one hundred of the Croatian parties will need to reassess and negotiate their ways into parties with broader appeal if they are to survive and/or play any real role in politics. Croatia is a country of fewer than five million people; it cannot support 110 political parties. Nonetheless, on our measure of tolerance, the Croatian party environment is an asset. It reflects an initial awareness that the arena must be open and competitive if democratic behaviors and ideas are to gestate.

A final example might well be drawn from Kosovo. It currently has twenty-two political parties, all with regional bases, narrow issue focus, and often constructed around individual personalities. Their platforms are intolerant, nationalistic, and inflexible as a general rule. Beyond that, suffrage in practice is problematic given the political and ethnic tensions that accompany the recent past and current military occupation of the wannabe state.

The nature of the political party system and the substance of political party activities provide dynamic insight into the thinking of central political forces in these countries. The menu of choices on the one hand and the extent of political negotiation and dialogue on the other are useful means of charting the direction of change in any particular system.

Broad Franchise

Still another useful factor is the measure of broadness by which the "constituents" are defined. In essence, how inclusive is the franchise in the political system? Limitations on the electorate or on citizenship will often reflect biases or impulses toward discrimination that lurk beneath the surface. These biases can resurface in times of systemic pressure or stress to undermine democracy. The definition of citizenship is an obvious manifestation of the degree to which the system is genuinely and irreversibly committed to democratic mechanics.

Croatia has taken the largest stride in this realm. It has genuinely broadened the franchise to all formerly hostile ethnic groups and built guarantees to enable participation. It remains only to facilitate the return of many Serbian people to their prewar homes to complete the process. The current leadership (Mesic et al.) does appear committed to this process. In 2003, Croatian President Mesic said at a state function in Belgrade (Serbia), "the return of refugees is a key for Croatia not only due to Europe but also for the country to prove it is a mature democracy."[8] Most of the other states in the region are making partial efforts (Romania and Bulgaria more than Montenegro and Macedonia). The difference among them, however, is not in direction but in levels of achievement. The worst examples are Bosnia and Kosovo. Both appear unable to forge such a commitment to a broad franchise. They appear to lack both the leadership and the credibility to make a move that would irritate the significant portion of the citizenry who remain physically and psychologically wounded by recent hostilities.

Rejection of "Nationalism"

Comparative studies have taught us that structures induce behaviors by both the governors and the governed. Yet it is also true that behaviors stemming from culture and circumstance influence the evolution of structures. This is the standard "form and function" relationship. We examine the political dynamics in a system as a way to understand how behavior and attitudes affect the journey toward a society's goals.

"Nation"

Identity and loyalties are essential to understanding any political environment. Given the range of examples with which comparative politics must deal, it is important to distinguish *nation* from *state*. American political rhetoric has rendered this difficult because it does not make this distinction. Simply, the sovereign state is a political entity, and one's identification with that political entity (in whatever form) is patriotism. The nation is an ethnocultural phenomenon. It is a group, often calling itself a "people," who in their mind are different from all others around them on a number of bases, such as race, history, language, religion, various concrete and amorphous cultural characteristics, physical traits, and preferences for food, colors, or music. If that inventory is not enough to distinguish a "people," myth fills the void. Typically, something is made up to distinguish "our people."

Because the state (the government) is assigned the task of providing for society (or at least providing the framework within which this can be done by other actors), one can make the case that it is naturally forward-facing. It has to think about tomorrow. In Southeast Europe, most of the societies are said to be "young"; that is, a very large percentage of the citizenry are not yet middle-aged. Most of the countries face formidable demographic problems: low or negative population growth rates, high death rates, and susceptibility to major diseases. Recognizing these hazards, some leadership groups in the region have made a systematic political effort to get the public to *face forward*. This effort involves placing much less focus on historical grievances and much more focus on what needs to be done to improve tomorrow. The attitudinal response to EU membership in the region has hinged on the ability of Southeast European leaders to bring their publics to ask the key forward-facing question: Will our future be brighter and safer in or out of the EU?

Anyone familiar with the history of Southeast Europe knows that the past is fraught with conquest, manipulation, and abuse of countries by their neighbors. It would be difficult to make a case that any country was without times when it was abused or without times when it did the abusing. History has been tangled and violent for this region of relatively small countries. In this historical context, nation and nationalism become important. Given a history where some "peoples" have made efforts to eliminate other "peoples" and in which political boundaries have never matched ethnic boundaries, *all* peoples have an inventory of grievances. To address those grievances, however, is to face backward. It requires arguing the rightness of "our" position and the wrongness of "theirs." It requires advocating "solutions" that can only be embraced at the expense of other groups, and that in turn creates more grievances. A focus on *nation* is always about the past. It is a feeling that binds "our people" together but only at the expense of isolating others. In Southeast Europe, that means driving the "others" out or eliminating them. Today, that drive has been called "ethnic cleansing." One is thus led to conclude that nation and nationalism are negative political phenomena. They block the political integration of a society and, building from an emotional identity, make political violence easier to rationalize.

What all this means to our comparative analysis is that it is useful and illuminating to gauge the level of nationalism (often labeled "ultranationalism" in this region) by focusing on how forward-facing or backward-facing a society is. The more the focus is on political performance and results, the less the public is likely to succumb to emotional arguments and backward-facing prescriptions. Although this phenomenon can be demonstrated in virtually every system in the region, the dominant illustration and the most devastating example is the nationalism that accompanied the breakup of Yugoslavia. That political arena has been gripped by violence and hatred from 1991 to this day, growing out of nationalist themes and the quagmire of history. Bosnia, Macedonia, Kosovo, Serbia, Montenegro, and Croatia today suffer in varying degrees from the legacy of recent violence. They are not alone in the transition from communism. Russia, Ukraine, Moldova, Estonia, Slovakia, and Hungary have all witnessed strong nationalist arguments that are most easily recognized when the political rhetoric dwells on the past. It should be clear that nationalism is an unproductive political phenomenon in the twenty-first century. Yet the notion remains controversial, especially among those embroiled in the recent violence. Nationalism's virulent manifestations in Southeast Europe are too numerous to inventory. Some examples that can be understood as typical follow.

Kosovo is the open political wound that is exposed and easily observable. It is an explicit example of ethnic politics and intolerance. Ever since the end of the Kosovo conflict in 1999, Serbs have retreated into small enclaves. Gracanica, in an area in the north and east abutting Serbia, is the center of this phenomenon.[9] Most Serbs do not speak Albanian and they remain fiercely loyal to Serbia. They continue to use Serbian dinars (the rest of Kosovo uses the euro) and they carry Serbian documents, while Kosovo's 1.8 million or so ethnic Albanians carry credentials issued by the United Nations. Serbs talk to each other on a Serbian telephone network. Because Kosovo is not (yet) an independent country, the Kosovo Albanian public piggybacks on the international prefix of Monaco. So, to talk to one another, a Serb and Kosovo Albanian must make an international call, even if they are close enough to see one another. Kosovo's ethnic Albanian-run government has declared that the Serbian network is illegal and has threatened to shut down the transmitters.

The main foreign powers (United States, United Kingdom, France, Italy, Germany, Sweden, Russia) currently managing Kosovo have decided that Kosovo will "soon" be an independent sovereign state. This decision is a dramatic reversal of their collective position in place since 1999.[10] This new posture was compelled by a Contact Group (the major powers cited above administering sections of Kosovo) realization that more than 90 percent of Kosovars were dedicated to Kosovo independence from Serbia. In the face of this recent NATO/EU/U.N./U.S. reversal, Serbs will be hard-pressed to create and legitimize minority autonomy or a semblance of minority rights in the new Kosovo. Serbs facing an assured discomfort in Kosovo are said to be "fatally depressed."[11] The future atmosphere is sure to be intolerant and the eventual departure of the European establishment and the United Nations will have left little model behavior. The mode of governing since the incursion of the foreign powers has been adeptly labeled "permanent crisis management." The death of the Kosovo president, Ibrahim Rugova, in January 2006 has contributed to the atmosphere of uncertainty.

Kosovo has huge economic problems, a chronic power shortage, high unemployment and weak (often nonexistent) rule of law. Paradoxically, recent surveys (analyzed in chapter 3) suggest that young people in Kosovo are the most optimistic in the entire region. An inviting explanation is initial naïveté.

The ensuing drama that will certainly unfold and refocus journalistic attention back onto Kosovo will come with this promised independence. The leader of Serbia's nationalist Radical Party, has declared that he and Vojislav Koštunica, Serbia's prime minister, have agreed that if Kosovo gets independence, it should be declared "occupied territory"—implying at best a confrontational future for the Balkan neighbors. Many would interpret this declaration as a public commitment to reconquering Kosovo.

The fallout from this scenario could set Serbia on a path away from European integration (NATO or the EU). It would then persist in the region as an embittered and isolated black hole in the center of Southeast Europe. Speculation is that NATO troops would then remain in Kosovo and the EU might feel compelled to continue to manage the province.

In contrast to the reality in 1999 when Kosovars were seeking protection from the assertive forces of the Serbs, the Serbs are now trying to hang on to their place in Kosovo. The Kosovo government-to-be and its minions are demonstrating their aggressiveness. The areas adjacent to the Serbian-Kosovar border (Preševo, Medvedja, and Bujanovac) currently in Serbia are inhabited by a mixture of Kosovars and Serbs (among others). Calls for referenda emanating from Kosovo on associating these lands with Kosovo have alarmed Serbs and the Serbian government. Since 2000, Albanian political parties have demonstrated considerable strength in these locales. This area has traditionally been unsettled, with rampant poverty and prolific black-market activity. Albanian nationalism has been strongly reflected in opinion polls since the early 1990s. Serbs then are appropriately anxious about rumors of partition and plebiscite. The Serbian government for its part has played the game both ways. It established a Coordination Body for South Serbia (2000) whose explicit task is to ameliorate ethnic and political conflict in the area. Still other "hands" in the Serbian government have been contributing to the tension with both rhetoric and threats.

International players, for their part, are wary of any effort to refocus politics in the region on ethnic principles or identities. This refocus could serve as the spark to reignite ethnic violence in many other venues in the region. The European Union Monitoring Mission in South Serbia has used the word "catastrophic" to describe such a move to partition the area ethnically.[12]

Cultural Sensitivity and Intolerance

The Roma, as a cultural minority, raise still another base for measuring tolerance. No more thorny and complex example of the role of cultural minority exists in the region. When Nazi Germany first embarked on its process of discrimination and genocide, one of the first targets was the Roma; the absence of reaction in Europe generally buoyed the Nazi regime's confidence in the acceptance of such intolerance. Studies suggest that the Roma have made some meaningful progress toward integration. Yet many distinct patterns of discrimination and intolerance continue to exist in and beyond Southeast Europe. For some Balkan Roma, the recent film about Macedonian Roma, *The Shutka Book of Records,* has reilluminated the problems. The documentary's portrayals are controversial precisely because they highlight the positive but stereotypical characteristics of the community. Specifically, the film represents Roma as cheerful, carefree, culturally different, and prone to behaviors different from the mainstream community. Perhaps most insightful and illuminating is a statement made in the film by a Roma spokesperson that "we Roma don't need a state because we have the entire planet."[13]

In a similar vein, official classroom Macedonian history has become a watershed issue. It illustrates the degree to which cultural and ethnic biases have crystallized (rigidified) in the thinking of Macedonians. In a clearly enlightened effort to provide balance and tolerance in the Macedonian educational system, teachers with varied ethnic backgrounds (especially Albanian and Macedonian) came together and crafted an account of the 2001 ethnic violence that pitted Albanian insurgents against Macedonian police. The result, entitled "Understanding Current History," was impressively framed by the Center for Human Rights and Conflict Resolution under the sponsorship of the Institute for Sociological, Political and Juridical Research in collaboration with the Helsinki Committee. Such sponsorship would normally establish the pedigree of the effort and legitimize it. Beyond that, twenty-five teachers from fourteen Albanian and Macedonian high schools worked for a year to get it right. To achieve balance, it included both conflicting versions of the events and a third interpretation that provides a synthesis of the two opposing views and deftly balances the lasting impressions of the episode. The need to address the questions of the younger generation effectively and constructively regarding a highly volatile and divisive set of events is obvious.

The episode itself lasted for more than six months, killed more than one hundred people and required international brokering to quell the violence. The ultimate agreement forged amendments to the Macedonian constitution that made minority rights more explicit. Dodging political grenades, Professor Violeta Petrovska, manager of the project, pointed out that participating teachers used "measurable, provable data" whenever possible. She maneuvered to say that the publication did not intend to replace an official version of events but was an attempt to present hard facts. Tellingly, she felt compelled to add, "The worldwide trend is to present students with facts, then they can reach their own conclusions."[14] This could be a classic case of reconciliation and positive evidence of growing tolerance in a society were it not for the significant Macedonian reaction among politicians, scholars, and "experts." They have complained that the product was "premature and counterproductive." They argue that such an attempt to analyze such a recent divisive episode will ignite more violence. Their position seems singularly self-serving and a blatant defense of the ethnic postures that have provided the underpinning for so many politicians and opinion-makers in the region today. The transparent threat of this curricular component is that it undermines the strident, emotionally driven, and ethnically whitewashed positions of some elites.

Elite Behavior

Clearly, those holding visible political positions in the system (as well as other highly visible elites in the society) must expect that their behavior will be seen as a model for the larger public. In this vein, interelite dialogue—tone and demeanor—are likely to generate ripplelike behaviors among others. Speeches and opinion-shaping that nurture polarization and zero-sum thinking can not only poison a political environment, but also fertilize intolerant behaviors and attitudes. This sort of milieu is ripe for nationalism and its propensity to victimize others.

On the positive side of the ledger, one finds the conduct of the Croatian president, Stipe Mesić. At the Twelfth Meeting of Presidents of Central European Countries (October 14, 2005), he modeled constructive behavior with both tolerant words and ideas. Excerpts follow.

> This [European integration] will create the first region—for Europe is a region on a global scale—where war as a means for pursuing politics will be excluded. A Europe of open borders and of the same rules and rights . . . One has to get used to the new realities; one has to learn to live in them and with them. . . . This is the first time Europe is integrating by the freely professed will of its states and peoples. Most Europeans believe in the project. . . . Neither should one allow lack of information, insufficient information or prejudice—which due to ill-fated heritage of the past, here and there we have not totally liberated ourselves from—shake the trust of citizens in a united Europe. . . . I do know that this very united Europe helps in creating conditions under which it will be possible to solve problems. . . . The very fact that the ratification process in parliaments has not encountered any difficulties but has at referenda confirms that politicians know what the issue is, however citizens do not really always know. . . . First, one should resolutely remove dilemmas and eliminate ignorance about what the European Union is and what it will be. Then, one should define perhaps even redefine the notion of Europe which is not solely a geographic or political concept . . . [it] marks the final outreach of European values, European tradition and European culture . . . inconceivable without Russia . . . hardly to be imagined without Turkey. . . . We are aware of the significance of this fact not only for us, but rather for the region, and we are also aware of the responsibility that we undertake in this context.

Yet another example is drawn from September 2003, when Mesić visited Belgrade, capital of the system with which Croatia had been entangled in a very dirty war just ten years earlier. In that "neighborhood war," twenty thousand people died and a quarter of a million people were displaced from their homes. It also triggered hostilities in Bosnia. The Serbian (then Serbia/Montenegro Union) president, Svetozar Marović, displayed great political courage, saying, "As a president of Serbia-Montenegro, I want to apologize for all the evils any citizen of Serbia and Montenegro has committed against any citizen of Croatia." President Mesić of Croatia responded with his own apology, "In my name, I also apologize to all those who have suffered pain or damage at any time from citizens of Croatia who misused or acted against the law." Marović and Mesić clearly modeled behavior at some political risk to themselves.

On the negative side of the ledger, the examples are legion. Bosnia, Kosovar, Albanian, Macedonian, and, to a lesser extent, Serbian leaders pepper most of their speeches and writing with poignant, emotive, discriminating rhetoric. Both the words and the values that underpin them would be appropriate targets for both quantitative and qualitative research. That research, once done, would most certainly illustrate the great distance that will need to be traveled before tolerance becomes a meaningful and operational value in the region.

University Design

Curricular design and value promotion and reinforcement can go a long way to implanting tolerant values and behaviors in generations of likely elites and other active professionals. If university components are organized in a hierarchical way and vertical communication is the norm, tolerance finds small quarter in the halls of universities. Signs of tolerance are few but can be found in important places in the region. For example, Bosnian universities—an important sanctuary for scholarly young people disenchanted with the war and its conflicts—hold out some prospect of modeling tolerant behavior. Banned from wearing headscarves on campus at their own country's universities, Turkish women are finding sanctuary in Bosnia.[15] Students say they are attracted to some universities because of their relaxed attitude to Islamic dress. In Turkey, students and teachers are forbidden to wear veils or headscarves at schools or universities. In Turkey, the campus is not the only no-go area for head-scarved women. They may not work in the civil service or parliament, or practice law.

In 2005 the European Court of Human Rights upheld the Turkish government's right to maintain the ban. Unlike Turkey, Bosnian law does not forbid women from wearing headscarves in public places. Additionally, Sarajevo's population is now largely Muslim and four hundred years spent under Ottoman rule means its local culture is close to that of Turkey. (Indeed, no other city in Europe so closely mirrors the culture of Turkey.) The university authorities, however, downplay talk of students coming to study there for purely religious reasons. "The doors of Sarajevo University are open to any person who would like to study here," said Zoran Seleskovic, secretary general of the university. One disincentive for Turkish students coming to Bosnia is that their diplomas are invalid back in Turkey. Degrees from Bosnian universities are not generally recognized outside of the country's borders. In Mostar, two parallel universities have been created, each accommodating its own ethnic population. Not only does this bifurcation contribute to a segregation of narratives and ideas; it also keeps the next generation of educated Bosnians separated socially, institutionalizing the ethnic separation and rationalizing the behavior of those that would divide society by force or politics.

The salience of this factor is understated here. Those working in universities know well how significant the shaping forces are that reside in university communities. The formative thinking that is nurtured and reinforced, in academic environments is significant and long-lasting. Values take shape, are reinforced, or are challenged and replaced in an atmosphere explicitly designed to contour thinking. Yet the pattern in the region is for universities to have changed only modestly since the demise of socialism. Curricular and faculty development require resources of both time and money. Most of the political systems, even with external support, have not prioritized university reform.

Immigration and Minority Policies

In environments prone to fear and discrimination, policies that confine or preclude target groups augur for protection. The subtext, however, is decidedly low on the tolerance scale. Protection of the majority will, in the special circumstances of Southeast Europe, quite inevitably victimize the minority. And that minority will lie in wait until it has the opportunity to reciprocate. A spiral is set in motion that ensures movement away from a democratic environment. These policies are quite easily observed and analyzed. The centrality of this indicator is underlined by the amount of energy the EU places in refining and reforming minority-related policies as it shapes the new union's common policy framework.

By 2007, Sofia faced the need to impose visa requirements on neighboring states as part of its accession to the European Union. Bulgaria, Serbia, and Macedonia braced to manage the consequences. Serbia and Macedonia seek to minimize the effects by declining to introduce visa requirements for Bulgarians, as would be the usual international practice under such circumstances. Bulgaria and Romania achieved EU membership in 2007 and were required to impose visas on Macedonians, Serbs, and Montenegrins in order to bring their border policy in line with other EU states. Bulgaria had many reasons to delay. In 2005, more than 415,000 Bulgarians traveled to Serbia and more than 230,000 went to Macedonia. Most Bulgarians traveling to Europe, do so by car, passing through Serbia.

Bulgaria also gains significant income from cross-border tourists. In 2005, more than 534,000 Serbians and 581,000 Macedonians vacationed there, according to statistics published by the Ministry of Culture and Tourism. While fewer Macedonians spend their holidays in Bulgaria, the number of tourists from Serbia and Montenegro has almost tripled in the last six years. Under EU rules, citizens of Macedonia and Serbia would have to obtain visas to enter Bulgaria. They could stay for a maximum of ninety days within a six-month period. To diminish damage that might result from the restrictions, Bulgaria scrambled to offer concessions to Skopje and Belgrade, including free short-term visa applications, one-year business visas, and speedy procedures for emergency cases. The EU may liberalize its visa regime toward Macedonia, which has been granted candidate status for EU membership.

Openness of the sort suggested by these maneuvers can be understood as an indicator of the "comfort" that systems have with movement across borders and "seepage" of populations from neighboring states. With the EU as a per-spective, many Balkan peoples begin to look and behave more like one another than when examined intraregion.

. . .

Tolerance manifests itself in many forms and with marked unevenness in Southeast Europe. It is the key foundation value that distinguishes democracy from other political manifestations. Without it, policymaking in democratic or transitional systems will be without a compass. Complex political decisions often pit one valid interest against another. In such situations, the system must have a core standard against which to check and correct its course. That "con-stant" should be tolerance if democratic development is the objective. The es-sential point is that mutually reinforcing patterns of intolerance are found throughout the region. As a complex attitudinal phenomenon, regimes will need to take strident, consistent, and affirmative action, first to stem, and then to reverse the pattern among both elites and masses. I have illustrated here that the phenomenon relies on many different variables. The intense examination of any one of them would prove valuable.

Chapter 3

Obligation

> *The freest government, if it could exist, would not be long acceptable if the tendency of the laws were to create a rapid accumulation of property in few hands, and to render the great mass of the population dependent and penniless.*
>
> —Daniel Webster

Searching for Public Sentiment

The "obligation" identified here is one that rests with the leadership of the political system. It is more than the effort to hear the disparate voices of the public. It requires that the system link itself to a value consensus found among the governed. But in transitional systems, as suggested, that consensus about basic social, political, and economic priorities and values is often absent. Communism ended with a sweeping challenge by both elites and masses. They had concluded in different ways and over different issues that the Communist system had failed to meet its obligations to the governed. "Movements" emerged whose synergy was simply what people were *against*. The clarity of the negative message was resounding, but the foundation for a *constructive* consensus was missing. These movements splintered and, in some cases, vanished when the debate began about what the public did want. Simply, the consensus was missing and, consequently, the nature and depth of the regime's obligation to reflect those values was problematic. Many of the political systems under scrutiny are still struggling to frame a constructive consensus.

The obligation to place publicly defined interests at the heart of policymaking is thwarted when those interests are so shredded and unclear. Politics in the Bosnian Srpska Republic is instructive. The 2006 toppling of Serbian Democratic Party (SDS) control of the legislature/government precipitated the rise of Milodrad Dodik, the new prime minister, and his Alliance of Independent Social Democrats (SNSD) in coalition with other opposition parties. The SDS had been dominant since the demise of socialist Yugoslavia. Dodik is a reformer in a place that has been lagging economically and isolated politically and socially since the end of the war in 1995. The fall 2006 elections demonstrated that leadership transition is unsettled and is managed by international actors, thus undermining the foundations of legitimate authority and long-term stability. Dodik may find his authority short-term and decidedly too little to address major reform challenges: creating an effective banking system rectifying privatization abuses, organized crime, and official corruption.[1] The very tentative coalition depends on support from minority parties of ethnic Croats and Bosniaks in the Srpska Republik, whose agendas demand more autonomy for local communities. Such legislation is on the books in the SR but all efforts to enforce the law have been frustrated. The singular focus of the prime minister's allies on multiethnic staffing of local government offices will undo the coalition and send tremors through whatever semblance of stability appears in the SR regime. The more strident members of the nationalist parties that compose the coalition will simply not accept the distribution of jobs among members of different ethnic groups. The SNSD has itself demonstrated little eagerness to set the wheels of enforcement in motion. Massive worker layoffs following the bankruptcy of the largest state enterprises will further contribute to instability.

Revenue available to engineer change is also a formidable constraint. A prominent political commentator assesses the reality this way: "All the balancing in the world can't allocate money that's not available, so it's beyond my understanding how the new government can provide for all [its pledges] within the restrictions imposed by international financial institutions."[2] Credibility falters when rhetoric blatantly diverges from reality. The promise to establish a special court in the Srpska Republic to ferret out organized crime and corruption has generated singular skepticism from lawyers in the system. Beyond that, they argue that "special courts" of any sort undermine the legitimacy of the regular judicial system and are inherently undemocratic. With the broader "community" pulling in so many different directions, how can political leaders meet their obligation to be responsive and tuned in? The answer may lie in the potential that surveying brings to the political environment.

Public Opinion Surveys

How substantial are the efforts at consensus today in Southeast Europe? Public opinion polls from the region suggest that although they are certainly not solidly formed, patterns are beginning to emerge. Generally, the number of Central and East Europeans who say that they have "some trust" or "a lot of trust" in government hovers at around 40 percent, significantly below the global average. Only Latin America and the Middle East have lower levels of trust in government. Trust in "the media" is around 50 percent, a figure above the global average and on a par with the highest levels in the world. When the World Economic Forum sponsored a survey in 2003 on the extent to which the public trust the legislature to operate in the society's best interest, 65 percent of Central and Eastern Europeans indicated little or no trust, and only 27 percent indicated some or a lot of trust. When asked if their country is governed by the will of the people, 70 percent of Central and East Europeans said no; 17 percent said yes. Curiously, more people of the region living in countries not committed to EU membership indicated confidence that their countries are governed by the "will of the people": 47 percent.

The International Institute for Democracy and Electoral Assistance embarked on a major study involving surveying in Southeast Europe. It partnered with the South Eastern Europe Democracy Support network, seeking to bring into focus two elements: (1) what democracy actually delivers to people and (2) perceptions of democracy as it is practiced in Southeast Europe. In its own words, it "sought to promote democratic reform agendas that are owned and established by local stakeholders."[3] There is little doubt that the execution of these surveys was conducted in the mode of *advocates* rather than critics. The IDEA study findings illuminate virtually all of the dimensions that have been associated in this volume with democracy. A review of those findings can provide very valuable detail. The responses and attitudes take shape in patterns that invite generalization. The study accommodates those who would search out fine detail by reporting even individual responses and focus group discussion.[4]

Problems, Causes, Solutions, Hopes

The surveyed public in the various systems reflected some meaningful differences; nonetheless, seven of the ten surveys included "unemployment" prominently as a critical societal problem. Corruption and housing also figured prominently in the thinking of most respondents. Croatia was typical, identifying unemployment and corruption as "main" problems. Serbs honed in on the relationship of the state to society. Montenegrins understandably saw "sovereignty" as the immediate problem and the "mentality of the people" as the longer-term problem. After unemployment and corruption, Bulgars identified poverty and inadequate social welfare as problems. Macedonians were typical, except they added "interethnic relations." Kosovars added "citizen security" and "ethnic violence" to our list. Bosnians in the Federation of Croats and Muslims conceptualized differently from their Srpska Republic (Serbian) counterparts. Federation citizens identified emigration, housing, nationalism and a nonfunctioning state as key, while SR citizens focused on the "unstable political situation." Overall, corruption and renovation of the mentality of people were recognized as the toughest problems to solve.

When queried about who is responsible for "solving" the above problems, the overarching pattern suggested the state (government) and its leaders. Croats focused on parliament. Montenegrins emphasized a partnership between leaders and masses with the EU providing the money. Macedonians responded most skeptically, suggesting that Macedonians will always wait for someone else to solve their problems. When pressed, they said that the state with a stable pool of experts should take the lead. Bosnians in the Federation (FBH) pointed to "younger politicians with outside help." Srpska Republic respondents said there are no "solvers," only powerful people driven by personal interests.

The caution displayed in responses about solving problems reflects Southeast Europeans' grasp of the root causes of the problems. Overall, they see their "mentality," their history, and bad policymaking as the norms. Kosovars and Bulgars were quick to point to vestiges of socialist mentality including collective irresponsibility. They also emphasize that there is inadequate understanding of democracy and how it might work. The Serbs (Serbia) and all of the Bosnians are drawn to the culpability of their politicians and "bad" policymaking, resulting in war and lawlessness. The Croats provided the most detailed responses. After gesturing to their heritage, they listed mismanaged privatization, lagging technology, and lack of capable managers as the causes.

The strongest sense about "solutions" hones in on structural change in government coupled with evolving attitudinal changes. The psychological focus was apparent in Macedonian and Kosovar responses. The structural emphasis is reflected in Serbian, Montenegrin, Bulgarian, and Bosnian (FBH) thinking. These include reducing bureaucracy, simplifying legislative processes, establishing sovereignty, enforcing the law, banning nationalist political parties, and "democratizing." Bosnians in the SR shared perhaps the most interesting vision, suggesting that their problems are too complex to solve in the near future. Theirs appears to be a very pessimistic vision and one not broadly shared in the region.

With all of this as background, the thousands of participants in the study were asked about their "hopes." The overwhelming modal response had an economic focus. Most mentioned both broad and specific things. In broad strokes, Croats listed peace, quality of life, choice, and the environment. Bosnians (FBH) hoped for the wisdom to replace war. Serbs sketched economic prosperity. Montenegrins wished for "opening to the world" and normalization. Bulgars wanted improved living standards. Kosovars sought political stability.

At the specific level, Kosovars hope for jobs; Macedonians, governmental reforms; Bulgars, more capable political leaders; Montenegrins, "more hopes than fears." Croats have the most detailed wish list: more respect for law, more political will for reforms, more political focus on "small people." As already suggested, people in the Bosnian SR respond that they are helpless and disillusioned. They would like to hope for a better living standard and no violent conflict but cannot bring themselves to hope for such "distant" things.

Access, Information, and Participation

Perhaps the most important single element of the IDEA study for this volume's concerns is the consistent and emphatic response of surveyed citizens from the entire region that elections are the *only* opportunity to have voice in their societies. Most also add that they have qualms about the degree to which those elections provide choice and voice. Croats share this skepticism with their neighbors; while acknowledging that in theory they have public opinion polls, media, and non-governmental organizations (NGOs) as options for participation, there is still great "distance" between people and politicians. Bulgars chime in, suggesting that no one is listening and elections are a facade. Macedonians do not brighten the picture. They say that elections should be important but that in reality the public are "absolutely marginalized." They argue that they get very few choices, fear reprisals given certain outcomes, and have no paths to participate other than elections. Serbs too say they have no alternatives for engagement other than voting and associate that option with the manipulation of political parties (which they hold in very low esteem). Montenegrins also insist that they have no "direct" way to engage except voting. Kosovars prefer to "not be involved in politics" (which carries very negative baggage and offers few opportunities to vote). Bosnians from the FBH say they have very little influence on the system, that elected politicians never meet expectations, and that the elected have no sense of obligation to represent their constituencies. Bosnians from the SR claim to have "no time" for political participation because they are consumed by challenges of "daily survival." Overall, then, the people of Southeast Europe are uniform in their belief that they have little or no opportunity to participate in the political system between elections—and many have profound doubts about the utility of voting in elections. The matter of nonparticipation between elections will be taken up in chapter 4.

The attitude regarding NGOs can help us understand why so many Southeast Europeans see few options for participation. In general, the countries vary in their civil society landscapes, yet even where NGOs are recognized to exist, they are seen by the public as operating in the shadows of the political system. In essence, they are viewed as tangential and powerless. Croats seem to understand best the role NGOs could play. They articulate support for NGOs and acknowledge that they could offer alternative ideas, educate citizens, and act as a vehicle to help the public "realize" their interests. Macedonians also imagine a role but insist they are uninformed about where NGOs exist. Serbians are the strongest proponents of NGOs. Their experience in 2000 when NGOs coalesced to successfully pressure Milošević from power no doubt is a major factor. The key player in that episode was an NGO named OTPOR, which was a grassroots youth organization dedicated to just one goal: Milošević's removal. Perhaps based on this experience, Serbs seem convinced that NGOs have the muscle to bring about changes in society. Bulgars too have some sense that there is potential in NGOs. They see the prospects most clearly at the local level; they believe that NGOs should be tax-supported and that NGOs are ready to engage but government is resisting. As a result, they give NGOs low marks for effectiveness. Bosnian FBH respondents see the NGO role as small and marginal, while Bosnia SR respondents argue there is no time in everyday life for such activities.

The Southeast European population has strong views about media and its role in society. They, like most modern people, rely on various media types and outlets for information. Public opinion about the media in the region is that it is untrustworthy; as a consequence, a citizen must engage multiple sources if one wants to understand the situation with some accuracy. The central concern stems from an impression that the content of the media is controlled by those who "own" it (this ownership issue is discussed in chapter 4). What follows is simply the public vision of the media. Kosovars trust only their domestic sources and dismiss all foreign media; the Bosnians (FBH), having had experience with a similar conflict in the recent past, seem to subscribe to the opposite idea. They distrust all domestic media and praise as objective the foreign media. Bosnians (SR), Serbians, Montenegrins, and Macedonians invest no trust in any media, insisting that one has to work hard via multiple sources to get close to the truth, and reluctantly seeing the independent media as slightly better than state- or foreign-owned media. Most see the media as tied in some fashion to either the political establishment (regime) or to the opposition. Some parties do have explicit ownership roles. Only the Croats see the media as a vehicle for participation by the public. Radio is seen as superior to print journalism. Croats also worry about ownership and control implications.

Images

In chapter 2 it was suggested that tolerance is essential to democratic development. This basic value must be consistent in the institutions of the system and must be reinforced by behaviors throughout the system. The following pages examine what the IDEA study has learned about images of ethnicities, religions, and neighboring countries in Southeast Europe. It is only a snapshot of opinions captured by a very refined and elaborate study. The political and violent wars of the recent past in Southeast Europe make it important to seek out a sense of the measure to which raw emotions and negative images are giving way to more normal images. We get some important clues from the IDEA surveys.

The good news for democracy is that no regional biases appear. Different publics seem to have different and localized images but victimization of a particular group on a regional basis is simply not indicated. Macedonians express some displeasure with "Albanians" and "Roma." Bulgars also identify Roma and Turks as sometimes troubling. Montenegrins are less prone to focus on ethnic or ethnonationalism than they are to focus on the tensions between the Serbian and the Montenegrin Orthodox churches. Serbs are comfortable with discriminating and negative ethnic images but are reluctant to specify or label groups. Pursued by a different approach, Serbs conceded that they have relatively positive images of Macedonians and Montenegrins and more negative images of Croats, Slovenes, and Bosnians. Similarly, Bosnians (SR) articulated that tolerance is an "officially sound idea" but acknowledge that there is no genuine commitment at the personal level. Bosnian (FBH) participants said that *everyone* belongs to a "national community," implying that they know the differences and live with them. This statement is a heavily veiled concession to the prominent place that ethnic and national identities hold in Bosnia. Montenegrins framed a positive position by suggesting that such images should be rational not emotional; if rational, one could be optimistic about co-operation. The Bulgars were most candid and forthcoming, indicating that Albanians, Bosnians, Kosovars, Macedonians, Montenegrins, and Roma are viewed negatively while Serbs are seen in mixed terms and Croats envisioned positively.

Any examination of tension and public hostility in the region would naturally turn to religious institutions. The linkage with national identity is one dimension; the political premise found in liberal, democratic systems of distance between church and state is the other. Religion since the demise of socialism has emerged as a central force in rationalizing behaviors and attitudes that have unsettled fledgling systems and often promoted and rationalized violence. In a conceptual sense, the notion that forms of Islam are the central problem in the region is misconceived. Were the parties able to step back and examine the larger developmental experience, they might understand that religion and democracy have intrinsic tensions and contradictions. At its roots, classic liberal democracy is grounded in the idea that man can define and pursue his interests in the framework of a tolerant and constrained political community. Religion, in point of fact, is a necessarily prescriptive and standard-setting phenomenon supported by a hierarchy with unyielding confidence in its own perceptions. Though it is possible for religion occasionally to promote a behavior or an attitude that is system-supporting in some political sense, the rationale is never consistent with tolerant, pluralistic liberal principles. The various peoples of Southeast Europe have come to recognize this discrepancy and have articulated their concern about the intimacy of church and state and the destination that that portends for society. Their instincts tell them that the church may prevail and, in so doing, neutralize the effort to develop democratic forms of politics.

With just one marked exception the generic response of citizens surveyed was that religion and politics—that is, church and state—in the region have become too closely connected, too intertwined. Croats suggested that the Catholic Church has embraced postures that can be seen as intolerant and inflexibly negative. Bosnians, though speaking often of different religions, seem agreed that the religions are too engaged in the politics and have, in the process, ceased to be value-driven. Serbs cling to the idea that their identity is linked to their religion but still conclude that the church (Orthodox in this case) is too much linked to the state and its leadership. Montenegrins claimed that the church is more "in service to politics than it is to religion." In Macedonia, the Macedonian Orthodox Church is given special political status and is shielded from incursions by even other Orthodox churches. Kosovo is the outlier. While not the only Muslim state in the region, it is the one with the most recent violence. The Kosovo survey suggests that citizens are very positive about the engagement of religion in politics. They asserted that "faith in God brings people together" and "in Kosovo religion is highly valued by all citizens." When independence is achieved, Kosovo will be an Islamic state and challenges associated with tolerance and constraint will follow.

Performance, Confidence, and Trust

The public perception of government performance is an important gauge of the obligation built into the political system. The mass public may be relatively unsophisticated about politics and government but they certainly know that government will do things to and for them. Their perception of that balance is integral to the creation of the latitude and the patience that all governments need from the governed in order to maintain order and a trajectory of development. The investigation we are using here approached this subject by inquiring about opinions regarding the best- and worst-performing political institutions and then inquired about the provision of public services specifically.

One salient finding is that political parties are evaluated very poorly and are perceived to perform very poorly by the Southeast European public. Croatians rated the executive leadership as the best-performing elements of government (president, prime minister, mayors) and pointed to political parties as the worst performing. Bosnians (FBH), given their circumstances, pointed to the "international community," local administrations, and mayors as the best. Again political parties made the worst of the worst list. Macedonians also see executive leadership in positive terms (president) and denigrate political parties and parliament. Bulgarians with surprising consistency said that no institutions performed well because "poverty distorts democracy." There is certainly a great deal to ponder in that statement.

The public services dimension should attract our attention because it reflects the popular vision of the most crucial day-to-day needs of the public. Utilities fare a bit better than other public services, and the most recurring criticisms are saved for "social assistance" or social welfare. Only Croatian respondents suggested that overall services were adequate. Pensions were the lowest-rated services provided by the Croatian system. Privatization was also attacked for not being sufficiently transparent. Bosnians (SR and FBH) were the most critical, suggesting that all services were poor but singling out social services and pensions as the worst and police and education as the best. Most thought that lack of funds was the cause of the poor performance. Most gave the leadership a pass on responsibility. Serbs said their military was the best and public transportation, social assistance, and health were the worst. Montenegrins, like many others, suffer from deferred maintenance and minimal reinvestment in infrastructure. Public transportation, the military, social assistance, and electricity are generally identified as the worst-performing. Bulgarians similarly pointed to social assistance, health care, military service, and heating, while giving electricity, education, and water positive evaluations. Macedonians touted electricity and heat and panned health and social welfare. The basket case of public services, Kosovo, nonetheless rated education and the army highly and social assistance and transportation worst. The picture in broad strokes is one of uneven and poorly performing public services in a region where the public, given the communist past, has been accustomed to the state providing cheap, minimal, and predictable (if not reliable and polished) services.

With this foundation sense of performance, we turn to confidence and trust. The bifurcated Bosnia is the most interesting case. Bosnians of the FBH place their highest confidence in the international agencies and organizations while their SR compatriots who are Serbian see the international actors as least warranting confidence. They place their confidence in the prime minister of their sector. But the Muslim residents of the SR share the FBH view that international players are worthy of high confidence and express least faith in domestic (SR) institutions. Serbs have high levels of confidence in their own future and are confident in the incremental path currently embraced by the regime. Montenegrins have an abiding confidence in their ability to recover economically now that they have achieved independence from their union with Serbia. Macedonians find most confidence in local political administration and leadership.

When the thousands of responses are filtered and separated, the pattern that emerges clearly indicates a lack of trust in political institutions. Political elites are the least trusted in Bulgaria, Montenegro, and Bosnia. Serbs are more patient, saying that the current personalities should be given time to earn the public trust. Croats are least trustful of political parties and local administration and are most likely to invest faith in the prime minister and local mayors.

The low public assessment of government's ability or inclination to provide goods and services for people is key to "trust" in these systems. One must recall the attitude carried over from socialism that it is government that has primary responsibility for providing goods and services to the public. This psychology of dependency is a major hurdle for transitional governments to overcome. The dramatic and persistent role played by external actors in the region's history also weakens the tendency for people in a system to have faith and trust in their own leadership. The record of empires, the cold war experience, the 1990s experience have all brought powerful actors into the region to "clean up the mess." Romans, Austrians, Ottomans, Soviets, the United States, the EU, the U.N.—all have contributed to a sense that the small states of the region are unable to manage their own affairs. People living in Southeast Europe have more often than not been required to choose which external actors they wish to support over any indigenous option. This choice has left "trust" an attitude without a sound foundation.

Governmental performance and history have conspired to weaken public trust in government in Southeast Europe. It must also be said that the quality of leadership itself—the uneven integrity and personal distance—has contributed to the thin levels of public trust. The region has also experienced violence at a level that certainly undermines confidence. The awareness that violence and war represent a failure of politics must inevitably redound to the image of political leadership.

Democracy

The most salient aspect of the IDEA studies for our purpose is the simple question about perceptions of democracy itself. The data are revealing and follow consistently from many of the ideas and perceptions cited above. Southeast Europeans (apart from the Slovenes, who have been in the European Union since 2004) do not believe that they are living in a democratic political system now. They do not believe that their systems are "democratic." The reports from the focus groups are very useful signals.

Of twenty-nine Croats in the focus group, twenty agreed that they do not live in a democracy. The absence of input mechanisms between elections is key. Serbs say that politics is still "chaotic." They see improvement since Milošević but nothing yet like democracy. Montenegrins claim that they are not living in a democracy and point to the "strong control" over politicians by the media, judiciary, and major companies. Macedonians simply lament that democracy has not yet congealed as a system. Bulgarians insist that there is inadequate public awareness of the "workings of democracy" to enable it to work. One resonating view is that democracy is freedom from any responsibility whatsoever. Thrusts toward democracy have been substituted with anarchy, lawlessness, and impunity. Bosnians make some of the most interesting assessments. Bosnians from the FBH share the view that the democratic system is good even though the concept appears ill-defined to most Southeast Europeans. They gauge that they have no real democracy; that they are at the very start of a journey in that direction; and that they are very far away. Bosniaks (Bosnia Muslims) think that they have more democracy than those living in other parts of Bosnia. It would be hard to validate that claim. The Croatian minority see their lack of representation as a sign of other than democracy and the decision by the U.N. high representative to replace their chosen candidate for "president" (Serbs, Muslims, and Croats each get to elect one of the troika) as validating the proposition that something other than democracy is operating in contemporary Bosnia. To that end, the Bosnians (SR) say they are "trapped between manipulations of local politicians and interference from the international community" that effectively neutralizes any impulses toward democracy that might have sprouted.

External Actors and External Appeal

The inescapable reality is that Southeast Europe is not alone in shaping its own destiny—political or otherwise. It exists and is transitioning in a globally dynamic, interdependent world where change presents itself at an accelerating pace. Information, people, products, and money wash across borders without interruption. Such rapid change would appear to make it an especially hard time to manage systemic transition. The region generally, but Bosnia and Kosovo in particular, have been targeted by international actors as destinations for high levels of political, economic, and military engagement. This targeting can enhance *or* constrain democratic development.

The IDEA research signals that Southeast Europeans believe the international community has a major influence on change in the region. Countries that are having greater difficulty—facing greater challenges—with the transition are consistently more positive about the role of internationals. Examples include Kosovo, Macedonia, Montenegro, and Bosnia FBH. Kosovars have concluded that the international community is essential for its reconstruction (some would argue initial construction) and NATO is viewed in the highest possible terms. Kosovars are certainly correct that without external funding and externally provided security Kosovo would not long survive. Macedonia is positive about the international role there but demanding. They insist on more flexibility for the Macedonian government in managing aid, more sophistication by those providing security, and less imposition on the Macedonian public agenda. They too praise everything associated with NATO involvement. Montenegrins focus their vision on the EU and the financial assistance it can bring. They relish the financial help and praise Europe as a stronger partner for assistance than the United States. They see the EU in benevolent terms and the United States as prone to conflict and often military conflict. Bosnia FBH believes the international community should play a major role and be open to what it conceives as "regional interplay."

The countries with a stronger record of reform and transition are more cautious about the role of the international community. Croatia, Serbia, and Bulgaria fit into this category. Bulgarians see the EU as a necessary step to take them in the "right direction" but attach little trust to the more powerful elements of the international community. The Serbs necessarily filter their views through the lens of the Milošević trial. It continues to perplex them long after it has ended and is reflected in a deep-seated suspicion about real international interests and intentions in Southeast Europe. Croatia too sees international engagement in the region in slightly positive but cautious terms. The Bosnia SR view bristles at the degree to which the international community controls the public agenda (although increasingly Serbs in the SR are finding more comfort with European engagement than with U.S. engagement). NATO is still largely perceived as an occupier. The Muslim minority in the SR fear a pullback by the international community and are pressing for Bosnia to join NATO.

The image of the international community is also affected by the pressures for emigration from Southeast Europe. The IDEA study reveals that emigration is still a modest pull for Southeast Europeans. The prospect of raising living standards or ensuring personal safety drive most decisions to leave. Macedonians say that they would emigrate to enhance personal safety, education, or career, but become reticent when they realize that the Macedonian educational system is often not recognized abroad. Montenegrins concede that opportunities for raising one's living standard could induce Montenegrins to emigrate. Serbs see escaping intolerance as a major motive. Bosnians FBH believe that a "large percentage" of Bosnians are prepared to leave if the opportunity presents itself.

Delegate or Trustee?

Can public policies be modeled on public opinion? Would the management of society be more democratic if it were to mirror "public wisdom?" The region is not without its struggle with these questions. To clarify, a decision-maker performing in a delegate role would perceive that an obligation exists to reflect the values, attitudes, and preferences of the public in the halls of power. A decision-maker performing in a trustee role would perceive that an obligation exists to exercise individual judgment on what is best for the community, whether this judgment matches the "people's wisdom" or not. In this scenario, the word "mandate" often surfaces, implying responsibility to go beyond or ignore the "people's wisdom."

Representativeness is another of those dimensions that Southeast European systems seem to have to work out in their own way. The experiences of many established democratic systems (including that of the United States) are unhelpful in marking the path. To reiterate, a delegate is a person selected by a constituency to mirror the views and perspectives of that constituency. The task in this mode is to reflect the vision and preferences of the segment of the public "represented." A trustee, in contrast, is also selected by a constituency, but perceives that the election was an endorsement of her vision of the issues; she presumes to make decisions based not on the public view but upon her own view. Such politicians often use the term "mandate" to signal their independence from public attitudes. Trustees often argue that this is "leadership." While it is possible to imagine a "representative" claiming to use both conceptions in "representing" a constituency, it is also likely that one or the other pattern characterizes the leader's behavior. The lack of clear commitment to one of these role models has clear implication for public voice and the public confidence in that voice.

Patterns of leadership in Southeast Europe indicate that the trustee interpretation is by far the most common among elites, although this should be understood as a matter of degree. Slobodan Milošević (Serbia), Franjo Tudjman (Croatia), and Alija Izetbegović (Bosnia) can only be labeled "supertrustees." By many measures they were authoritarian in their political behavior. Many others have demonstrated an arrogance that can best be understood as a trustee mentality framed by an electoral mandate.

Such arrogance is hardly warranted. Since the transition from communism began, the collection of new political systems (in all of Central and East Europe) have held fifty-nine general elections. Fifteen of those were "first" elections. Of the forty-four elections in which incumbents were running (that is, second or third elections), thirty-four resulted in the opposition winning. In one sense, this could be interpreted as a good thing. That elections have come to be a reliable mechanism by which to change leadership is the good news. The bad news is that such pendulumlike swings from party-in-power to party-out-of-power and back again derail strategic policymaking and interrupt step-by-step construction of a societal design.

More subtly, it may be that this pattern is a function of a kind of transitional logic. Many analysts have speculated that in the more politically developed countries in the region, there is a constituency for those in power, a second constituency against those in power, and a third constituency that remains skeptical that elections will actually bring a change of leadership. To be clear, they aren't sure that those in power will give up power even if voted out. For those voters, their only option is to vote for the opposition because only then will they be able to test the system; that is, find out if those in power will give up power. Some speculate that this subset of voters ranges from 5 percent to 15 percent in the countries of Southeast Europe and as such may tip the scales consistently to the opposition vote.

The foundation of democracy is soft if these central questions are left unaddressed. Obligation requires clarity of principle to which one is obligated. All persons are "obligated" to something or someone but democracy requires that the obligation to the electorate or larger citizenry be defined. Only in this way can leadership be held to standard. Only in this way can those in power understand their commitment and obligation.

Macedonian Health Policy and Public Opinion

The Macedonian health drive targeting smokers is an illustrative example of the concept of obligation, and its application by the trustee.[5] The motive of policymakers may be to improve society, or it may be to jump on the EU momentum for banning smoking from public places; clearly, however, it is not a reflection of current public values regarding tobacco use. In classically Balkan form, Macedonia passed antismoking legislation more than ten years ago and only in 2006 has begun to enforce the law (and then only in the capital). The law prohibits smoking, advertising, and selling cigarettes to those under eighteen. Fines are heavy: the equivalent of thousands of U.S. dollars. The tobacco lobby is credited with the long delay in enforcement, but the enforcement problem stems from the reality that the rules are very unpopular. More than 50 percent of the adult population of Macedonia smokes. The percentages for children are lower but significant. The ambiguity of policymakers contributes to a public sense that democracy is eroded or perhaps was never established. In a fledgling democracy, the public draws its sense of what democracy is or what they can expect from democracy from such examples of trustees-generated policies. Worse, the credibility of policies is challenged by the nonenforcement of some policies. If nothing else, this sort of political dilemma demonstrates how difficult creating patterns of working democracy can be. The point is that *forming* obligation and massaging the ways it does and does not take root in the political system are awkward and uncharted paths for these transitioning states.

Institutional Principles (Constitutions)

It is relatively easy to make the case that socialist Yugoslavia was key to the instability in Southeast Europe in the 1990s. Yugoslavia was technically and functionally a federal system. More conventionally designed communist systems were unitary systems. Among the communist political systems that were "federal systems" (Soviet Union, Czechoslovakia, and Yugoslavia) there was an appropriate skepticism about the degree to which lower-level decisions were insulated from the central authorities. The reason that the distinction is significant at all is that all of the so-called federal systems from the communist era disintegrated with the transition, whereas all of those that were unitary have retained the same political boundaries. Perhaps the fact that they were nominally federal systems indicated the disintegrative pressures that existed when the three systems were formed. In any event, it strongly suggests that communist systems were particularly inept at forging new bonds and identities that could hold a diverse political system together under stress.

Compounding this problem in postcommunist states, communism made no effort to create a public understanding of the workings of the political system. Guiding one's behavior in it based on the constitution would have produced great frustration or worse. In simple terms, constitutions did not and do not automatically generate traction in the political thinking of publics in communist or postcommunist states. Political experience in communist systems simply taught people to frame political expectations by other means and to seek other logics by which to engage themselves with government. The Southeast European systems emerging from communism set their constitutional direction toward participatory, representative, and open governments with varying measures of oversight, limits on authority, and transparency. The variations are significant, but the thrust was decidedly toward Western-style constitutional systems. All have written constitutions.

There were advantages and disadvantages to the relatively fast or slow paths to constitutional design and approval. All of the postcommunist constitutions are less than two decades old, and the transition has put great strain on all of them. Limited resources, ambiguity, complexity, and thin public knowledge have hampered the patterned growth of predictable behavior by both government and nongovernmental actors in these political systems. In essence, they are not yet institutionalized constitutional systems.

Constitutional Issues

Three basic issues have drawn and will continue to draw the attention of political scientists as they scrutinize the theory and practice of the new Southeast European constitutions. The first is the effort to define "community." That is, who is entitled to be a part of the society and what protections are afforded the majority and minority? The effort is seen in provisions about official language, eligibility for citizenship, and minority rights. These issues are particularly thorny. The second issue is the impulse away from pluralistic, federal styles.

The communist legacy and the inexperience and anxiety of new leaders, coupled with the disintegration of "federal" Yugoslavia caused many makers of new constitutions to tilt away from decentralization of political power. The last issue is, in many ways, the most crucial and the most enduring: the issue of sovereignty. The new Southeast European constitutions faced and continue to face political strategies linking them to the European Union, which necessarily abridges that sovereignty. EU member and candidate states effectively join a macrostate that has, even if it chooses not to exercise it, sovereignty over the populations in the member states.

In Bosnia, most of 2005 was spent in a broad-based effort to recast and reform what should be called Bosnia's preconstitution. Begun on the tenth anniversary of the Dayton Accords and with the expectation that results would be clear by March 2006, the process had the impetus of the Bosnian leadership. The talks ended in utter failure in January 2006. International voices as well as political leadership from eight political parties fell silent without any progress. The process has been critiqued from many angles. One central shortcoming appears to have been the apparent exclusion of the general public either by way of input or by way of assuring transparency. One assessment notes, "The early stages of the talks were veiled in secrecy, a fact that scarcely contributed to any sense of 'ownership' by the general public."[6] The international community has also been pressed to shift much of its attention to Kosovo as its future presents some immediate challenges.

The current arrangement (which is hardly institutionalized) divides Bosnia into a maze of complex and overlapping cantons, districts, and other political units. The U.S. Institute of Peace (USIP) that hosted the talks was insensitive to the appearance that the United States was again imposing its own design on the Bosnians. The appearance of strong management (some say manipulation) was reinforced by the role of American Don Hays who had previously served as deputy to Paddy Ashdown, the U.N. high representative and longtime supergovernor of Bosnia. Both nationalists and many others who had hoped for a more genuinely and singularly Bosnian dialogue resisted the external guidance. U.S. and EU efforts were perceived as pressing. Sensitive to this perception, Hays underscored the Bosnian party leaders' role and emphasizing the United States Institute of Peace as facilitator.[7] The more typical perception was that of Srdjan Dizdarević, president of Bosnia's Helsinki Committee. He suggested, "This is a matter to be resolved by us. . . . The only outcome will be ill fortune if the international community again determines our fate."[8] He went on to suggest that constitutional reform would not be effective until the country's mentality was changed. "At present only half the population is proud to be citizens of Bosnia and Hercegovina."[9] He claimed that many Bosnian Serbs and Bosnian Croats do not identify with the country at all.

The primary issues remained unresolved. Parliamentary reform to restructure and empower the legislature was key. There was also a recognition that the rotating tri-presidency is dysfunctional. Some effort was devoted to framing a system that would not violate the established European Charter. A short list of the unresolved issues indicates just how basic the discussions and disagreements were:

- Method of presidential elections
- Method of electing the House of Peoples
- Representation of minorities in parliament
- Legislative mechanisms for policymaking
- Authority of many government structures
- Inability to create and implement policies that are EU preaccession requisites

There is little debate that without increased government effectiveness and centralization, Bosnia will have little chance of taking the first step toward EU membership. Without the constitutional reforms suggested by the list above, no "stabilization and association" agreement is possible. The collapse of the process then is consequential both in the short and long terms. Resistance to centralization was evident from many quarters but the representatives of the Srpska Republic were particularly entrenched. Haris Silajdžić, head of the Party for Bosnia and Herzegovina, framed the enlightened position, saying, "What we need is a civil democracy . . . the ethnic principle, forced upon Bosnia by the genocide that took place in the country, is unnatural."[10]

Legislation

In politics, the machinery produces policies, decisions of all sorts, judgments, and prescriptions. These are the things that come out of the back end of the political machinery. The raw materials (that is, what goes into the front end) include information, opinion, strategies, calculations, and more—all filtered by the design of the machinery. Both elements should be kept in mind as we frame opinions about, and assess the performance of government. The array of factors that one should examine to fully understand a political system is nearly endless.

It can be argued that hasty legislation may be worse than no legislation at all. Such an example is found in Bulgaria's haste to generate agricultural policies in advance of EU membership. With less than a year to meet EU benchmarks, the Stanishev (socialist) government was bent on fulfilling all commitments especially in agriculture. Food standards and implementation mechanisms were lagging and were of particular EU concern. The legislative response to this game of catch-up was to try to move forward on legislation on as many as six different tracks at once. Animal husbandry and food processing were two especially complex realms where the EU was acutely sensitive. Without effective legislation, the farmers felt vulnerable to, say, avian flu or any similar uncontrolled development. The Bulgarian system also lacked enforcement capability to deal with substandard food processors. Hasty legislation had resulted in an awkward multiplication of unanticipated problems. Reticence to legislate created other issues. The narrow time frame for finding legislative solutions to an expansive range of problems placed stress and images of nonperformance on many of the new governments in the region.

Financial resources are also pressing on Bulgaria. Their commitment to adjust and improve their monitoring of the economy comes at a major initial cost, flying in the face of Bulgaria's commitment to repay IMF loans and to reduce government spending overall. Legislative debate has also been diluted by an effort between the ruling coalition and the opposition to collaborate in order not to "feed Euro-skepticism."[11] The Bulgarian example demonstrates that, especially when legislation is considered, policymakers have many masters to serve. If the public holds a view of a less than enlightened type, should democratic "representatives" mirror their views in the halls of power? The easy answer is no or only to a point, but that begs the most awkward question: at what point is the system no longer democratic?

Obligation is one of those requisites that is hard to measure because it is so frequently a part of the political rhetoric. It is also awkward because those political systems that pretend to be models of democracy are hard-pressed to prove their commitment to it beyond their own political rhetoric. As a central operational value in any political system, "obligation" underscores the necessity of long-term recognition that value platforms exist without enforcement mechanisms or structural compulsions. Rather, they reside in the judgment and values of the individual leaders and in the community of those exercising authority. It is a common illusion to think that a political system could by its rules and structures "obligate" leaders to behave in this democratic mode. New regimes that make this mistake find themselves entangled in what is most often labeled corruption, which reinforces public skepticism. At its heart, the problem is the naïveté that imagines that obligation can be built into a political system in short order.

Chapter 4

Voice

The citizen who criticizes his country is paying it an implied tribute.
—William Fulbright

Perhaps the answer to the question posed in chapter 3—at what point is a system no longer democratic?—is that voice need only be heard, not reflected in public policy. Perhaps if people perceive they have power, it is enough. Voice in politics would seem to be a simple thing until it is examined carefully. It then becomes a maze of issues and questions that pull in different directions. Does the voice of the majority need to be articulated? Does the voice of the minority need to have impact? Is there an obligation, once heard, to accommodate or mediate voice? When voices change, must policy change? If there is no majority voice, should the modal voice prevail? Is voice diminished if orchestrated by the authorities? And finally, does the intensity of voice matter?

One of the longest-standing examples of voice can be found in the call by the Transylvanian Hungarians for autonomy. Romanians outnumber Hungarians in Transylvania by a factor of four (1.5 million to 6 million). The Romanian government struggles with the call for autonomy and the interests that underlie it. The issue leaves both sides raw and has in the recent past generated violent and deadly protest. One recent articulation of this objective came on March 15, 2006, when a council representing some Hungarians "demanded" action by the Romanian government to grant autonomy. Tension seemed exacerbated by the new Romanian media commitment, consistent with democratic norms, to report on controversial issues. Ultranationalist groups on both sides have seized the opportunity to raise their own visibility, vowing to fight to defend their positions. The Romanian parliament had earlier rejected such pressures, declaring that autonomy based on ethnicity was "anti-democratic and anti-European." The issue is made more awkward by the Romanian constitution, which claims Romania is a "national, unitary and indivisible" state.

The episode in the spring of 2006, nonetheless, passed without violence because Romanian President Bašescu entered into a dialogue with Hungarian spokespersons and the tension was drawn back into the realm of routine politics—a clear example of a regime recognizing the obligation to give voice to issues and to acknowledge its value in the system. From the Hungarian side, statements emerged underlining that these interests residing in the Hungarian community in Romania would be pursued "only" in a democratic way. The Romanian Institute of Marketing and Polls has measured a rising degree of acceptance by Hungarians of the long multicultural and multiethnic history of the region.[1] Other Romanians are less open. Hungarian groups working through coalition strategies in and with mainstream Romanian political parties have gained concessions in education, local administration, bilingual signs, and media ownership.

Constituency Relationships

In the last chapter it was suggested that "obligation" necessitates clarity about roles and what is often called "representation." Thinking about "voice" reminds us that *how* the obligation issue is resolved directly impacts on one of the capacities for voice. The conventional notion that formal institutional channels for voice are embedded in the elected official is problematic. Perhaps far more crucial are the channels of communication placed at recognized places in the bureaucracy. Often what citizens need or want from the political system is not new legislative policy. Rather, the average citizen is far more likely to be looking for a small-scale decision or interpretation. Often this takes the form of a basic service, a clarification, or an acknowledgment of some small need or idea. To accomplish this successfully, citizens require a "map." The map will provide guidance as to the design of the system and the functional differentiation within it. The map will provide enough information to identify where responsibility for "concern x" resides. Effective voice, then, is problematic in political environments that either do not have a refined political architecture or that have not routinized the responsibilities to the point that one could know "who does that." Moreover, the political system must be constructed to ensure it possesses "ears" to hear what is being articulated.

Still other avenues can exist that can bring voice to issues by less direct means. Media channels, social movements of various sorts, financial contributions, or essentially nonpolitical relationships can, in given situations, make the public *voice* more resonant. Many of these are taken up in the following pages.

The Montenegrin Independence Gambit

Montenegrin independence was and is an acute tension in the region. Symbols have appeared that reinforce the formally achieved independence. A statue of a former king and a flag attached to that era bolster the current government's political posture. The official flag is a decided reflection of eras passed. With just over half a million people, Montenegro has pushed to join the proliferation of ministates in Southeast Europe. After World War I, Montenegro was folded into the new Kingdom of the South Slavs (which in 1929 became Yugoslavia). The current struggle—thankfully more political than violent—was resolved in the May 2006 referendum on independence. The "Whites" favored remaining in union with Serbia; the "Greens" pushed for independence. Clearly, the Greens prevailed by a modest margin. The republic's foreign minister, Miodrag Vlahović, argued, "If there is any vote in favour of independence, one thing is clear—the state union won't exist any more. If we have any majority, the state union is over and done with."[2] Indeed, that is what happened.

The EU, seeing the implications more clearly, had established both turnout and margin of victory requisites on the outcome. Unless those thresholds were met, (50 percent of registered voters; 55 percent voting yes for independence) the EU would not recognize the mandate. The Montenegrin regime interpreted these prescriptions as favoring rejection of the pro-independence effort. The Macedonian foreign minister said, "They [EU] have 'incentivised' and favoured one side—the very antithesis of democracy."[3] The thresholds were met and independence was the result. Montenegrin independence has become the reality. Clearly, Brussels was and is concerned that, coming on the heels of Kosovo's moves toward independence, Montenegrin independence would be unbearable for Belgrade.

Montenegro had already become a distant partner of the Serbian-led union. It dumped the dinar used in Serbia for the euro, removed signs and symbols referencing the state union, and conducted its own diplomacy. Montenegrin officials had even proposed (unsuccessfully) to discuss the division of assets and resources before the vote for independence. Montenegro is a sharply divided area with just 42 percent of the population identifying as Montenegrin and 35 percent identifying as Serbian. Concern focused on whether Montenegrins would vote their ethnicity and how the remaining groups (Muslims, Albanians, and Croats) would divide themselves on this issue. The prospect that "nationalists" could come to power in Belgrade (the Radical Party) was thought to tilt the Montenegrin minorities to the government's independence position. Emotions and political intrigue ran high. The opposition parties insisted that the Montenegrin regime (Djurkanovic) was authoritarian and corrupt.

One credible position articulated during the debate was that Montenegro's fastest route to the EU is with Serbia. Many see independence setting the clock back and lengthening the road to EU membership. The government argues that it will get special consideration as a newly independent state.[4] Further, it proffers that Montenegro cannot be worse off than it is; without Serbia, Montenegro will be what its people can make it be—not more, not less.

"War Criminals" and Public Opinion

The death of Milošević while on trial in the Hague has reopened debate about the necessity and wisdom of turning indicted persons over to the international tribunal. Though the focus is on Mladić, Karadžić, Tolimir, Župljanin, Hadžić, and Djordjević (the highest-ranking fugitives), the reality is that many others may be affected from Serbia, Bosnia, and Croatia. For the tribunal's part, they insist that they will remain dedicated to bringing the prominent "war criminals" to trial in spite of their ability to elude capture for more than ten years. The stalwart position of the EU and the tribunal may be unrealistic, given that full cooperation from the Southeast European states would be requisite to achieving this goal. Officially, the contemporary regimes are committed but broad internal support for such a commitment is fleeting.

Mladić is rumored to be in Serbia and the regime is not on record denying that. Karadžić is presumed to be in the region though perhaps not in Serbia proper; Serbia, the Srpska Republic, and Montenegro are seen as likely options. International pressure on Serbia continues for the arrest of Mladić. The EU has linked integration talks with official Serbian cooperation. The emerging image of Milošević the martyr, however, reduces the likelihood that the Serbian authorities (Koštunica's government) would prioritize international pressures over large-scale public sentiment. Increasingly, the Serbian public sees the tribunal's conduct as illegitimately slow, unreasonably halting, and without moving to any "meaningful" resolution.[5] A politician's worst nightmare: the nearly even split between those favoring sending Mladić to the Hague and those who find such an action unacceptable. The EU has set and ignored its own deadlines for capture and handover, significantly weakening its own hand in the process. The last was April 5, 2006.

The political solution in the face of such a basic public split in opinion is perhaps obvious: proclaim cooperation and remain inactive. Such a strategy is not only pragmatic but finds some foundation in the Dayton Accords language. For politicians in the region generally, this topic is a lose-lose issue. The official position of the Srpska Republic is that those indicted should turn themselves in. Serbia has sent sixteen of those indicted to the Hague only after they surrendered voluntarily.

Efforts have been discussed to open more military archives, search for records of action in Kosovo, search for associates and locations, and establish a new task force that could help apprehend Mladić. Many believe that the Stabilization and Association Agreement (SAA) represents the first significant step toward EU participation. In that sense, it represents both hope and despair for many Serbs. Both agree it will be a long road. EU member states may also take independent positions on the SAA, with Serbia slowing or halting the process altogether. Such was the pattern established with Croatia's application and the thorny issue of the apprehension of Ante Gotovina.

Women as a Constituency

The data below suggests that Southeast Europe has started to make political leadership more accessible to women (see table 1). The socialist period left a mixed legacy on women's roles. Socialist Yugoslavia, compared to other former socialist systems, accommodated larger numbers of women in politics in both formal and informal roles. The data in table 1 reveal a start has been made. Legislatures reflect women's representation to be between 10 and 20 percent. Some may find the position of Slovenia a bit of a surprise. It is not at the forefront of the trend; Bulgaria, Serbia, Croatia, Macedonia, and Bosnia have all committed impressively to the opportunity for women candidates. One could easily suggest that all of the Southeast European states have embraced the possibility of the leadership of women, at least in the legislative realm.

Centralization

The next design feature that draws our attention is the center-periphery question: How will power be distributed between the central authorities and the various levels of authority in regions and districts? This is one of those "architectural" issues that needs resolution before voice can be accommodated. This centralization-decentralization issue requires an analysis of the trade-offs well recognized in political science. With centralization comes a concentration of power that may be abused, but that also brings consistent policy to the whole

TABLE I
Women in Southeast European Legislatures

Country	Seats/Total Seats	Percent
Bulgaria	51/240	21.25%
Serbia	50/250	20.00%
Croatia	27/152	17.80%
Macedonia	21/120	17.50%
Bosnia	7/42	16.70%
Slovenia	11/90	12.20%
Romania	37/331	11.20%
Montenegro	9/81	11.1%
Albania	10/140	7.20%

Source: Current embassy and legislature Web sites. Also see: http://www.idea.int/gender/wip_handbook.cfm.

system. With decentralization, decision-making is closer to the people who are likely to be affected by policies, but there is also the potential for inconsistency in the implementation of policy. There are of course many more implications to the center-periphery question. The bureaucracies associated with the old communist systems did not simply go away when communism collapsed. Vast numbers of bureaucrats, with tendencies to do things just the way they did them in the past remain, fought for their own survival and resisted reform or change. The common discomfort of democratic political leaders in transitional systems stems from the belief that to "break the stranglehold of the bureaucracy," leaders must have more centralized power and authority, even if their ultimate goal is to decentralize power. The public climate for this centralization is often negative and skeptical. For most, it seems to move away from accommodating voice and away from democracy.

Another dynamic part of this political picture concerns the points of access for public input to government deliberations and policymaking. As the political architecture changed fundamentally, Southeast Europeans were told that they now had access. They now had a role to play as members of the political community. But the political systems generally did not provide maps to the public on how to navigate the new political architecture. In essence, the public was left unclear about where the doors and windows were for gaining access to government. Besides the channels for access, the public needs to know where power and responsibility lie within the government so that access to the right person or agency is possible. Unless those who wish to advance their interests know which part of government is responsible for particular functions, the result is likely to be "access" without impact—clearly, a prescription for frustration.

Civil Society

The overarching challenge in the development of civil society is to nurture grassroots political activity in Southeast Europe that could become the basis for widespread, genuine public participation. This participation would pressure each system to become more responsive to the public voice. It could rebalance the delegate-trustee pattern of representation. The concept of civil society is very much in vogue today, but it suffers in Southeast Europe from some ambiguity as a concept. There is considerable debate about which actors can be said to be a part of civil society. Do business interests fall in the mix? Do organizations that are created or supported by commercial interests fit? Do religious organizations come under this rubric? Do organizations initiated with or receiving significant public funds fit the label?

When the EU surveyed the Central and Eastern European countries that have recently become members, it concluded that much more needed to be done to enhance and nurture civil society and it committed resources to the task. But the new member states mostly responded by using the resources to provide local organizations and movements with a menu of items and services that could be provided or financed by the central government using funds provided by the EU. The fundamental problem was that simply by generating the menu of policy positions and an inventory of fundable assets, the central government was conditioning the form and nature of the issues at hand. An alternative view argued that this was counterproductive. What was needed was for the local constituencies themselves to decide on what their issues were and what they thought they needed to further their interests, thereby forming a genuinely grassroots, bottom-up process. But that would likely produce (1) some inept requests for support, (2) some very localized and insignificant efforts from both the central government and EU perspectives, and (3) some efforts that could become a challenge to the plans and directions of the central government. For these reasons, the more manipulative approach was and will likely continue to be the norm. Perhaps the more neutral term "guided approach" would better represent the establishment vision of this dilemma. There is evidence that all of the new Southeast European states wrestle with this question and, to date, resolve it in a standard and uninspired way. Civil society in Southeast Europe today thus appears more robust than it actually is. Many genuine efforts are evident but they are narrowly defined and superficial in support. The lesson from Southeast Europe may be that there is no way to accelerate the development of civil society meaningfully without castrating the effort. It must be a self-generating and self-perpetuating phenomenon if it is to contribute meaningfully to democratic development.

Kind of Participation

The overwhelming expectation in the public's political psychology is to anticipate that government will solve problems and provide services. Very little evidence is yet apparent of groups forming to activate their own energy and resources to solve problems. This inactivity should be interpreted as a part of the legacy of communism reinforced by patterns in developed societies where resources have driven such expectations. One is hard-pressed to identify groups in the region that, in an autonomous manner, establish what they think is needed and resist turning to government for assistance or guidance.

The issues around which most local energies are focused include social services, schools, minority rights, unemployment, and economic development zones. Most such efforts reflect a general disaffection from political parties as a vehicle for promoting these interests. While difficult to establish definitively, this disaffection appears to be both a spontaneous aversion and a result of chasing EU funding in most of the countries in the region.

Elections as Political Art

The salience and sheer weight that political analysts ascribe to elections are formidable—surprising given the voluminous literature on election irregularities and manipulation in new political states. The mainstream argument is that competitive elections are a necessary and sufficient indicator of democracy. Any alternative to elections is less constructive and less democratic. Perhaps so, but the reality that must be acknowledged in Southeast Europe is that elections are more clearly art than science. In the worst cases, they reflect the normative and prescriptive thinking of those managing the transition. In the best cases, they represent warning signals to those same elites. What the world sees and what Southeast Europeans see certainly differs with the experience and political sensibilities of each population.

First among the problems is the designation of *constituencies.* Where and how the boundaries are drawn and how the electorate is defined or qualified predestine the outcome. Post-Dayton elections in Bosnia come to mind as keen examples. Even in classic, established democracies, the preelection identification of constituencies is a partially visible process at best and is a locus of significant power struggles.

Second are the *choices.* The range and representativeness of the candidates and the policy choices color the attractiveness or acceptability of the elections. Given the absence of an established civil society and the reality of thinly rooted pluralism, the menu is, at the very least, directed by those with power. In the worst cases, war-validated political groups (most often paramilitary groups) and externally sponsored groups tend to generate the electoral choices.

Third, in the *absence of pluralism,* political parties have abbreviated and uncompromising platforms. "Ideological" parties reject pragmatism and the mass appeal that compromise and inclusion could generate. The nature of some of these ideological parties is intimidating and aggressive. The tone is often polarizing rather than consensus-building. The most strident elements of political parties portray a "single truth" aura that will serve democratic development very poorly.

Fourth, voter *turnout* is problematic. The overall pattern in the region reflects a decline in voter turnout with each passing general election. Aside from common boycotts of the sort seen in recent Montenegrin and Kosovar elections, a more elemental issue exists. Elections are understood as the moment when the people's voice identifies the direction for the country and chooses who will wield authority. What is missing from this perception is the notion that elections are only one stage of an *ongoing, participatory process.* Many countries in the region have a record of electing persons who behave in an authoritarian way after the "democratic" election. A political psychology emerges in which successful candidates imagine themselves as "supertrustees," as opposed to delegates with continuous obligations and links to the constituency. The supertrustee perception draws policymaking away from compromise and real dialogue. The primary responsibility for this pattern lies with the leadership. Their inclination to see public input as complicating their jobs or making less clear the direction for public policy is at the root of the issue. Even those with a delegate mentality are prone to feel under pressure from the tasks at hand, resulting in their turning away from regular public input. Less tangible but certainly a factor is the unspoken qualms that leaders have in the "wisdom" of the masses. These qualms are compounded by the rationale that the leaders "know" what the people want.

Nonetheless, the impetus for change is the responsibility of the public. They must assume that only by generating pressure for responsiveness will a regime allocate time and energy to the input processes. In the absence of established political values that "obligate" those with authority to listen constantly to their political environment, leadership from elements in the civil society must materialize and persist. A relatively easy and workable structural adjustment that could set a positive process in motion would be the creation of multiple ombudsmen—roles filled with high visibility and highly respected personalities. Once in place, the obligation to listen to them and give *their* sense of issues that have traction serious weight in the policy deliberation process should follow.

Fifth, the gaps between elections are characterized by closed or narrowly *constrained input mechanisms* in the system. There is a view that a voter by voting buys a ticket and sits back and experiences the ride. A more constructive view, but one that is hard to find in Southeast Europe, is that elections are one kind of input but that democracy requires regular elite-mass interaction and significant efforts by leadership to account for both popular and minority interests. The crucial notion here is that democracy requires that the process be consistent and ongoing. Elections represent a snapshot of voice and participation but are altogether inadequate as a platform for public input.

The overarching point here is not that elections are counterproductive. To the contrary, they forge some support and are certainly a part of democratic political evolution. But without evolving awareness of the limits and imperfections of elections, and without genuine interest on the part of the leadership in unpopular views, elections remain a less central feature of politics than the commitment to developing civil society. Elections are art in the real sense that Southeast Europeans will see what they want to see in them—positive and negative. They will not assuage political anxiety.

None of the above argues for ignoring elections. Rather, it suggests an approach that anticipates the limits of elections and the likely public response to them. Former U.S. Deputy Defense Secretary and World Bank president Paul Wolfowitz, commenting after a May 2003 trip to Bosnia and Kosovo, suggested that those places hold lessons for American efforts to bring postwar stabilization and the transition from dictatorship to democracy in Iraq and Afghanistan. He concluded, "The experience in Bosnia shows the danger of rushing to hold elections simply as a show of democracy taking root. The threat is that dangerously divisive leaders may be the first to take power. By holding elections so early, it became impossible to remove some bad actors, because they now had electoral authority."[6]

International IDEA identifies a number of "major problems" regarding elections and participation. Their inventory includes:

- Weak electoral administration in terms of ethics, professionalism, and deficient election legislation;
- Interference by state authorities in the election process;
- Unreliable voter registers;
- Elections that are not fully representative;
- Low-level organization of civic and political interests, especially those of women and minorities;
- Ineffective political parties and political institutions that are unable to formulate and reflect the interests of various groups at the public policy level.[7]

Their analysis adds this dimension: "In addition, inequality and de facto discrimination based on gender, ethnicity and religion are a source of conflict in the society. The region's weak democratic culture does not have mechanisms to manage such conflict and promote democratic governance in respect of multiculturalism. Widespread poverty worsens the problem."[8] Some recent volumes add incite on a broader comparative level: *Comparing Democracies 2: New Challenges in the Study of Elections and Voting* (Thousand Oaks, Calif.: Sage, 2002), edited by Lawrence LeDuc, Richard G. Niemi, and Pippa Norris; *Electoral Systems and Democracy* (Baltimore: Johns Hopkins University Press, 2006), edited by Larry Diamond and Marc F. Plattner; and *Elections as Instruments of Democracy: Majoritarian and Proportional Visions* (New Haven, Conn.: Yale University Press, 2000), by G. Bingham Powell.

The recent Macedonian election is a relevant example. The Macedonian parliament, under pressure from the EU, visited the issue of campaign financing. The need for placing limits on campaign spending by political parties and appropriate enforcement was recognized. Continuing talks on Macedonia's progress toward EU membership ("candidate" status as of December 2005) would hinge on Macedonia's commitment to EU rules on campaigning and campaign financing. The tension in Macedonia's case stems from the financial limits being so low as to invite violations. The law prescribes a per voter amount that applied to a modern campaign becomes unworkable, given media and other campaign expenses. One international monitoring group, Transparency International, estimates that spending easily exceeds four times the legal limit.[9] Audits suggest irregularities with bank accounts, account-keeping, and reporting. The primary watchdog unit, the State Anti-corruption Commission, lacks any power in this realm. A consensus exists that political parties operate in a "gray" zone. To date, no political party has been penalized for campaign funding violations. Renata Deskovska, a prominent law professor, asserts that an entirely new body might need to be set up to monitor election expenses, in order to "be aware of the amount of money spent on campaigns, determine its origin and ensure the names of all donors are made public."[10]

Sources of funds are naturally a matter for special focus. Suspicions that economically powerful individuals are linking donations to influence on legislation are commonplace. Of particular concern are designs to inhibit reforms that would open the economy to fair play standards or to reforms that would reduce the oligarchs' (post-Communist super rich) insulation from prosecution. Deskovska concludes, "It's no secret that they expect something in return in the form of benefits, privileges and tenders."[11]

Structure and Ownership of Media

The centrality of the media in any discussion of "voice" is a given. Bosnia generates a perplexing example of external efforts to support articulation via the media. The Bosnia war damaged virtually all aspects of the media. Buildings, equipment, resources, the psychology of journalists—all suffered significantly. The very fabric of journalism is destroyed in the civil wars we witness in the world today. And indeed, journalists emerged playing a significant role in the incitement of hatred and ethnic division in postwar Bosnian society. The journalists' sense of professional fraternity was fractured. Journalists became transmission belts of propaganda and volatile political ideas, mimicking the new political circles of power that emerged from the former Yugoslavia. State television was split three ways into ethnically focused and highly interpretive "news" channels—mouthpieces for the Serb, Bosniak and Croat warlords. Independent media were co-opted, attacked, marginalized and eventually silenced. With the Dayton Accords, "guns fell silent" but the war of words escalated in the newly segregated media milieu. It was in this atmosphere that so much attention was directed to international intervention in the resuscitation of the media in Bosnia.

Estimates suggest that more than $100 million has been sent to Bosnia from external sources to assist the development of the media.[12] Donors and recipients agree that the fallout from these efforts is disappointing. Likely, the media, like the larger political system, is still divided ethnically in the wake of the 1990s. Journalistic standards continue to be low and little progress has been made in the media to ameliorate ethnic boundaries and tensions. One summary assessment claims, "A decade on, the media market in Bosnia and Hercegovina remains ethnically polarised. It is also heavily influenced by political parties and remains financially dependent on donations and on often unethical advertising."[13]

Local Bosnian assessments ring familiar. They tend to claim that international donors were rather naive, inexperienced, short-term–focused, and insensitive to local media-related ideas and needs.[14] They also seemed to expect that they could generate instant interethnic dialogue. Senad Avdić, editor and chief of Slobodna Bosna, reflects the mainstream sentiment: "The international community came in without much regard for local ideas and needs. Instead they tried to replicate the media scenes from their own countries into a completely different society. . . . They thus created 'monsters' which sucked up their money and could never stand on their own feet, while at the same time they ignored truly local voices and initiatives."[15]

Some improvement is evident. Nationalism and related hate language have lessened. The incitement of hatred has diminished in the mainstream media (albeit unevenly in parts of Bosnia). Ironically, media experts and practitioners have concluded that in neighboring Serbia and Croatia, where far less support from the international community has been channeled, more progress has been made in professionalizing and introducing standards to the various media.

International donors conceded mistakes in the initial rush to provide assistance. Some allocations were channeled to "highbrow" publications with virtually no circulation. The premise underlying such allocations was that real change could only come about by reshaping and influencing the intelligentsia. Donor coordination was minimal. The common ideologically expressed goal was to promote regime change and democratize society but there was little shared sense of what that meant. In Serbia, Milošević provided a common target for change. No such focus existed in Bosnia. Postwar Bosnia was characterized by massive international intervention, splintering, resistance to coordination, and nation-building in lieu of state-building. American and European efforts clashed. American donors tilted toward private media outlets and European efforts concentrated on public service outlets, resulting in some duplication and much waste. Both sectors suffered.

By 2000, four million Bosnians could seek information from 210 radio stations, 71 television channels, and 130 print sources.[16] One critic observed that this was a strange strategy akin to a "curious mixture of capitalism and Maoism" embodied in the slogan, "Let 100 flowers bloom." Open Broadcast Network alone absorbed $20 million and in four years could not win over enough news viewers from the state broadcast networks to make itself viable. To survive, it became an entertainment channel. Some were hopeful that a British Broadcasting Company (BBC) consulting team operating in Bosnia from 2002 to 2004 might be able to engineer improvement to the overall media environment for news. To date, the changes are stalled. The upbeat analysis[17] claims that broadcast news is more independent than print news. It also suggests that a legal framework is in place that could reintegrate broadcasters. A systemwide channel exists that nearly all Bosnians could tune into (Bosnia Hercegovina Public Broadcasting System, August 2004). Yet ethnic stations still dominate news. Reform is unsupported by elites as well as the masses. The BBC plan remains unimplemented by either Bosnian politicians or international donors. It is labeled as just another plan from outside Bosnia. Donors were fatigued and politicians judged the plan unrealistic. BHTV1 was created with a thin budget and a resistant public in the Srpska Republic. The EU attempted to put some impetus back into media reform but failed.

The Serbian experience with rebuilding the media is complex and typical. Serbia's TV and Radio B92 have managed to create a more positive position, recognizing the need to compete in an open marketplace of ideas. While external aid helped some outlets survive regime change, it proved unable to sustain them over time. The money placed in the development of the Serbian media drew more results than similar funds invested in political party development or NGOs. Serbian political parties that replaced Milošević have displayed many of the nondemocratic impulses and qualities that motivated their ascension. NGOs with muscle have joined political parties while others have languished with poor leadership or have succumbed to various pressures from the government. The Serbian government still perceives these organizations as antigovernment elements. Among the media that have maintained their roles as "authentic" watchdogs with a democratic commitment are B92, Danas, and Vreme.

One reason that it has become so difficult for Serbian media to do their jobs stems from the period immediately following the demise of the Milošević regime. The new democratic forces apparently expected that the substantial support they received from media when they opposed Milošević during the struggle for power in Serbia (2000) would carry over into the new administration. Such "unconditional" support was not forthcoming. In their proper democratic role, many media outlets critiqued the new administration's behavior, generating some of the same abrupt responses toward the media that had characterized Milošević's regime. The unfortunate result was a splintering of the reformers who had managed to wrestle Milošević from power. The media position resonated with local politics in Serbia, resulting in a disconnect between local and central governments. Those foreign donors still in the environment tended to side with the central government, financially undermining the integrity of independent journalism in post-Milošević Serbia. This dilemma has also resulted in no reform-focused media legislation that would support, validate, or protect a democratic, independent, and competitive media.

The few surviving media players in Serbia today reflect their ability to anticipate the changes in the environment in which they are operating. For them, "sustainability" was the central organizational goal. Many sought expert input especially focused on professionalization of journalists and refinement of financial and managerial skills. The result was a laserlike focus on social responsibility for journalism and an equally intense strategy for financial viability, including long-term financing. They also broadened the range of their activities. Radio and television were linked, Web sites were added, CD labels were created and modest publishing houses formed. It is clear that throughout Southeast Europe, no state subsidies will be allotted to independent media. If state-run media can be converted to public service media, the proverbial "playing field" could be leveled.

All this means that anxiety levels among media managers and analysts remain high owing to the concern that the essential values underpinning a functioning democratic media have not been built into Serbia's political system. The implications are far-ranging; from a practical perspective, however, the most immediate and significant is that many potential investors are reluctant to invest until such guarantees and regulations are in place. B92 is the only privatized media company in Serbia today that is viable. B92 was careful to preclude the state from becoming a major stockholder and carefully screened investors, using a value-focused litmus test. Management was concerned about "oligarchs"; that is, tycoons who might want to influence editorial policy in a way that would protect their gains from war-related commerce. It also distributed shares to employees with the provision that these could not be sold outside the company and established a "trust" to oversee stockholder maneuvers. These elaborate maneuvers are a tactic to insulate B92 from government influence. It is believed that the government sees the privatization of the media as a process in which government is losing a measure of control over public information and has chosen to move at a glacial pace on reform as a consequence.

Bulgaria also provides examples of strain in the development of the media. In late December 2005, the Bulgarian parliament passed some media-related legislation buried as an amendment to the state budget for 2006. It has shaken the media community in basic ways and portends to impact the entire information environment dramatically. Bulgaria has issued systemwide broadcasting licenses since 2001. Commercial broadcasters found revenue in advertising while the two state-funded public media corporations existed on the state subsidies. This situation abruptly changed when the government changed policy, allowing the public stations to broadcast as many commercials as do the private stations. This freedom essentially represents a tenfold increase in the advertising permitted on state-run networks. Combined with the €50 million annual subsidy, the two information giants in Bulgaria became "monsters." In essence, the policy allows state-run networks to compete for advertising revenue with private, commercial networks. Bulgarian National Television and Bulgarian

National Radio (state-subsidized) have primary market position in Bulgaria; the fears are that advertisers will be drawn to those outlets, leaving the commercial networks (BTV, Darik Radio, Nova TV) without enough support to maintain themselves—in effect, to kill the private media outlets. Both public networks have been criticized for accommodating the regime's interest; in this sense, the demise of the private news sources could have dramatic impact on the news and the public's voice.

Critics point out:

1. the radio and TV advertising market in Bulgaria is only € 100 million and to date represents a "fragile" balance between public and commercial media;
2. the change will allow total domination by the big two, destroying market competition;
3. the change violates European competition policies;
4. under the Amsterdam Treaty (1999) state financing of public broadcasting cannot damage the competitive environment for media organizations;
5. the change was imposed without any consultation with the media community;
6. the policy turns the clock back fifteen years and takes Bulgaria further away than ever from European "best practices."[18]

The media in Southeast Europe is challenged to play catch-up in many ways. The war and its consequences, along with the political disintegration of Yugoslavia, and the legacy of the various forms of socialism in the region have resulted in fifteen years of relative isolation and propaganda that has left a rather fractured informational environment. People and governments are challenged to rethink their senses about the media and its role in each society's voice. Journalists too have behaviors to overcome. Many have embraced self-censorship as a mode. Systemically, infrastructure is costly. The legal and regulatory systems are not in place. Investigative journalism is essential if journalists are to play their roles in a democracy but is also costly and can involve personal risk.

As if all that were not enough, journalists in the region have a responsibility to deal with the unpopular features of the recent past—politically, socially and morally. To accomplish this, journalists need to be protected by their organizations and by the central authorities. Further, journalists in Southeast Europe will also have to tangle with the realities associated with minorities. Ethnic, sexual, political, and linguistic minorities have issues that journalists will need to examine for and with the public. Such examination will be uncomfortable, in many cases irksome. Journalists will need more protection and understanding from the general public as well as the authorities. All of this suggests that the project of institution-building must include the media as a central feature in a democracy. The process is not in place, nor have the political commitments been made. It will certainly not be easy. Perhaps the most accurate notion is that reform will require genuine political will that is not yet in evidence. Hopeful signs are found in Serbia's B92, Croatia's *Feral Tribune,* Bosnia's MREZA PLUS, Montenegro's Vijesti, and RTK (Radio Television Kosovo) in Kosovo. Democracy requires more good news. An impressive analysis that speaks directly to the ownership and decentralization issues of media in democracies is C. Edwin Baker's *Media Concentration and Democracy: Why Ownership Matters* (New York: Cambridge University Press, 2007). It also contends with theoretical visions of how journalistic responsibility and "bottom line" considerations should interface in a democracy.

On balance, it is clear that major changes are in the works: some owing to internal guidance from media executives but others from external technological change. Media organizations face opportunities as well as competition from blogs, the Internet, digital television, and satellite transmissions. Per Byman, Swedish media expert, draws this conclusion, "The media success stories in the Balkans are all based on strong local media organizations that were able to attract foreign funding through inventive strategies and a lot of risk-taking—both financially and politically. The failed projects are those that were started or promoted from outside, with little or no local support . . . those who should survive have probably done so. And the others? Well, it's too late to do anything about them now anyway."[19]

Party Membership

Membership in political parties can enhance voice but only a heavily mediated message can penetrate and survive the "party" process. Ideological political parties (cadre parties) may exclude so-called out of range ideas. Mass political parties will most often moderate or neutralize ideas to the point of nonrecognition. For these reasons and because political parties in Southeast Europe are in their infancy and are most often single candidate–focused (that is, organized around the candidacy or personality of a single individual), political parties do not play a major role in manifesting citizen voice in the region. If and when they become vehicles guided by a complex of policy positions or ideological principles, their role could both deepen and broaden.

Demonstrations

It should be added that the dramatic transition from communism has also resulted in a significant number of people in many of the countries who do not accept the wisdom of the path toward the market system or toward liberal and participatory democracy. Meaningful questions must be raised about their "voice." Protests and demonstrations continue to be viewed as regime-challenging and worrisome. Little evidence exists in the region that would reinforce the "demonstration" as a vehicle for effective voice in politics. This situation will need to change: protest can be a relatively clear channel for articulating concerns or demands, especially those perceived as urgent. As a technique, the demonstration avoids the static of so-called mediating organizations.

Voting Behavior and Electoral Systems

Table 2 provides a glimpse at the structural features of the electoral systems in Southeast Europe. A clear pattern emerges with only a few outliers. Six of the eight systems (Montenegro was not yet independent when the data was collected) use the classic proportional representation system.[20] Though the sizes of the legislatures vary, only Bosnia has a decidedly smaller number of seats (forty-two) in its legislature. Albania uses a more complex dual system.[21] Serbia has no provisions for direct elections. The dominant system for election

TABLE 2
Table of Balkan Electoral Systems

Country	Electoral System for Legislature	Type	Tiers	Legislature Size	Electoral System for President
Albania	MMP	Mixed	2	140	—
Bosnia and Herzegovina	List PR	PR	1	42	FPTP
Bulgaria	List PR	PR	1	240	TRS
Croatia	List PR	PR	1	151	TRS
Macedonia	List PR	PR	1	120	TRS
Romania	List PR	PR	1	345	TRS
Serbia and Montenegro	N	—		126	—
Slovenia	List PR	PR	2	90	TRS

Data last updated: January 2005. *Source:* International IDEA. Stockholm, Sweeden. Drawn from world data set: http://www.idea.ing/esd/world.cfm.
FPTP: First Past the Post
TRS: Two-Round System
List PR: List Proportional Representation
MMP: Mixed Member Proportional System
N: No provision for direct elections

of the executive (president) is the Two Round System. Five of the states use this common system where, if all individual candidates fail to get a majority of voter support, a run-off election is held between the two top finishers in the first round. Bosnia uses a "first past the post" system, which means that whichever candidate gets the largest number of votes wins.

The election data for legislative and executive elections follow (see table 3). They create a portrait of general "enthusiasm" for elections. Examination of the data will reveal that in 1996 the Albanian election saw more persons registered to vote than existed in the voting-age population. In 2001, more people voted than were in the voting-age population. In fact, 120 percent of the voting-age population voted! In Bulgaria, the data shows every legislative election (1991, 1994, 1997, 2001) involved more voter registrations than people in the

TABLE 3
Election Data: Legislative Elections

	Total Vote	Registration	TV/Reg	Voting Age Population	TV/VAP
Albania					
1991	1,963,568	1,984,933	98.90%	1,985,550	98.90%
1992	1,830,000	2,000,000	91.50%	2,051,430	89.20%
1996	1,963,344	**2,204,002**	89.10%	**2,193,030**	89.50%
1997	1,412,929	1,947,235	72.60%	2,228,430	63.40%
2001	**2,468,000**	N/A	N/A	**2,040,574**	120.90%
Bosnia					
1996	1,335,707	2,900,000	46.10%	2,572,520	51.90%
1998	1,879,339	2,656,758	70.70%	3,256,197	57.70%
2000	1,597,805	2,508,349	63.70%	3,053,221	52.30%
Bulgaria					
1991	5,694,842	**6,790,006**	83.90%	**6,736,500**	84.50%
1994	5,264,614	**6,997,954**	75.20%	**6,501,110**	81.00%
1997	4,291,258	**7,289,956**	58.90%	**6,414,519**	66.90%
2001	4,608,289	**6,916,151**	66.60%	**6,391,816**	72.10%

(continued)

TABLE 3
(Continued)

	Total Vote	Registration	TV/Reg	Voting Age Population	TV/VAP
Croatia					
1992	2,690,873	3,558,913	75.60%	3,591,750	74.90%
1995	2,500,000	**3,634,233**	68.80%	**3,464,230**	72.20%
2000	2,821,020	**3,685,378**	76.50%	**3,484,951**	80.90%
2003	2,520,008	**4,087,553**	61.70%	**0**	N/A
Macedonia					
1994	707,210	1,222,899	57.80%	1,477,980	47.80%
1998	793,674	1,572,976	50.50%	1,621,599	48.90%
2002	1,241,605	1,664,297	74.60%	0	N/A
Romania					
1992	12,496,430	16,380,663	76.30%	16,408,080	76.20%
1996	13,088,388	**17,218,654**	76.00%	**16,737,320**	78.20%
2000	11,559,458	17,699,727	65.30%	18,597,776	62.20%
Serbia/Montenegro and Slovenia					
1992	1,280,243	1,490,434	85.90%	1,497,000	85.50%
1996	1,136,211	**1,542,218**	73.70%	**1,499,960**	75.70%
2000	1,116,423	**1,586,695**	70.40%	**1,543,425**	72.30%

Source: International IDEA, Stockholm, Sweden, http://www.idea.int/vt/parl.cfm. Collected from individual country reports, 2000–2002.

voting-age population. Similarly, Croatia in three of four legislative elections also registers more voters than it has. Romania and Slovenia in 1996 and Slovenia in 2000 demonstrate the same pattern.

If the data on executive elections are examined, the same pattern emerges (see table 4). In seven of seventeen presidential elections (two in Bulgaria and Croatia; one each in Macedonia, Romania, and Slovenia) the number of registered voters exceeded the number of those in the voting-age public. If one

TABLE 4
Election Data: Presidential Elections

	Total Vote	Registration	TV/Reg	Voting Age Population	TV/VAP
Bosnia					
1996	1,333,204	2,210,189	60.30%	2,366,000	56.30%
1998	1,879,339	2,656,758	70.70%	3,256,197	57.70%
2002	1,298,811	2,342,141	55.50%	0	N/A
Bulgaria					
1992	5,154,973	**6,857,942**	75.20%	**6,405,000**	80.50%
1996	3,358,998	**6,746,056**	49.80%	**6,440,280**	52.20%
2001	3,784,036	6,889,638	54.90%	0	N/A
Croatia					
1992	2,677,764	3,575,032	74.90%	3,591,750	74.60%
1997	2,218,448	**4,061,479**	54.60%	**3,450,370**	64.30%
2000	2,589,120	**4,252,921**	60.90%	**3,484,951**	74.30%
Macedonia					
1994	1,058,130	1,360,729	77.80%	1,477,980	71.60%
1999	1,120,087	**1,610,340**	69.60%	**1,438,948**	77.80%
Romania					
1996	13,078,883	**17,230,654**	75.90%	**16,737,320**	78.10%
2000	10,020,870	17,699,727	56.60%	18,597,776	53.90%
Slovenia					
1990	1,153,335	N/A	N/A	1,498,500	77.00%
1992	1,280,252	1,491,374	85.80%	1,497,000	85.50%
1997	1,064,532	**1,550,775**	68.60%	**1,495,460**	71.20%
2002	1,050,533	1,610,234	65.2	0	N/A

Source: International IDEA, Stockholm, Sweden, http://www.idea.int/vt/pres.cfm. Collected from individual country reports, 2000–2002.

could account for those discrepancies without altogether discrediting the election process, the trends suggest significant and impressive voter turnouts in legislative elections, except for Bosnia and Macedonia. Bulgaria, Romania, and Slovenia reveal declining voter participation in executive elections.

As suggested in chapter 3, Southeast Europeans perceive elections as their primary (and, in many cases, their *only*) opportunity to raise their voices in the political system. Until important mechanical issues associated with registration and voting are resolved in these systems, one must remain cautious about the efficacy of elections. At the very least, the responsible interpretation of these data is that, if elections are the channel for the voice of the people in a democracy, the "line" in Southeast Europe is rife with static. The clarity of the people's signal is problematic and government efforts to reinforce credibility with refined procedures in elections are deficient.

In chapter 3, I suggested that obligation is difficult to institutionalize. In contrast, I suggest here both explicitly and implicitly that voice can be built into the structure and functions of the political architecture of the system. Given that, it is easier to "see" the phenomenon taking root in Southeast Europe.

Chapter 5

Constraint

Government is not the solution to our problems; it is our problem.
       —Ronald Reagan

The conceptual underpinning for constraint is found in the basic notions of classic liberalism. The state should contain its impulses to encroach on the individual while managing the collective affairs of the whole population. Seeking that balance, the authority should tilt in the direction of constraint; that is, *not* expanding control simply because one can.

Collateral Respect for Opposition

Conflict has sharpened the political positions in Southeast Europe, and recent memory contributes little to the notion that respect for those out of power is both a wise and necessary function of democracy. The carryover political instincts from the former communist regimes reinforce the need for this transition. In the communist regimes, becoming a "political loser" was tantamount to a political obituary. Because the Party was seldom challenged (and still less often defeated), it became natural to portray and treat all "losers" in a denigrating way. They were routinely marginalized, discredited, and disappeared. The sense was that they had an "incorrect" vision of the future and therefore were impediments to progress. This idea has been quite resistant to change in the postcommunist period.

Many are reluctant to run for office; preferring to avoid the possibility of losing. Others learn from recent experience that losing can place one in real physical jeopardy. The opposition in Albania, Kosovo, and Bosnia have experienced violence and intimidation after losing power or failing to achieve it. Implied in these apprehensions and behaviors is the notion that the opposition has no credible role to play in policymaking and governing. Realistically, these systems must recognize that they will need all the human and intellectual energy and resources to address their issues effectively. When the majority "speak" via elections and a government is formed, quite simply, it does not cancel out the ideas, values, and prescriptions of those who were supported by fewer voters.

Transition of Power

In a political system that values the transfer of power in response to public signals, the role of the opposition must balance its desire for power against the reality that its behavior can, if unconstrained, erode policy effectiveness. From a policy perspective, with the transition from one regime to another, some measure of consistency is essential. In broad terms, this consistency is the balance between system maintenance and adaptation that all systems must seek. Those in authority and those aspiring to be in authority must recognize and respect the rules (limits) imposed by the design of the system. The political architecture must reinforce political behaviors associated with leadership transition that create a credible, meaningful role for the loyal opposition. The opposition, in turn, must accept the constraints within which system-supporting dialogue can be framed and policies made. The most obvious source of problems may be campaigns and the packaging of campaigns. Even in refined democracies, opposition and regime cadres seem unable to say that the other political postures are credible and are worthy of serious consideration. In the effort to provide a vivid "choice," voters in aspiring democratic systems are often presented with stark and mutually exclusive packages of ideas that tend to try to locate themselves 180 degrees from their competition. This polarization can and does veil options for mixing and matching policies based on their integrity rather than on their political sponsorship. It can severely reduce the policy flexibility of those in authority and certainly reduces the likelihood of stable, strategically focused public policies. The absence of this sort of constraint undermines the process of negotiation and compromise that are so much a part of democratic policymaking and implementation.

Controls on Police and Bureaucracy

The police and bureaucracy are the two elements in society most likely to impact a common person's life. Attitudes about the political system will stem from encounters with these elements more than from anything else, including the top political leadership. Constraint then in the behavior of the police and bureaucracy is critical to the public's vision of politics. These are the two most prevalent environments for "corruption" simply because they are best positioned to leverage their power over common people. For this reason, democracies, if they are to enlist the legitimacy and support of their publics, must curb the inclination of those with opportunity to exercise power in their own personal interest—financial or otherwise.

While structural remedies—including sufficient pay for such officials—can reduce corruption, it is essential that an ethos germinate (by honor or some other value) that confirms and reinforces constraint among those with opportunity. Once developed, this value consensus must be translated into a legal code with disincentives and significant consequences for breaking the law. Postcommunist political systems, if they are to claim democracy as their platform, must take explicit steps to scrutinize the behavior of police and bureaucrats and *publicly* hold them to account when they abuse their power.

Law and Politics

There is the matter of creating a new legal framework. A legal system obviously becomes the guide to behavior for the general public, for commercial activities, and even for the government. Without one, there are no rules of the game by which to judge risk and reward. Without one, the environment is unpredictable and vulnerability rules. "Corruption," whatever meaning is given to it, finds operating space in such a setting.

In this realm of the transition of postcommunist political systems, one encounters the greatest levels of misunderstanding among citizens, political leadership, and analysts. The form of social control under the communist system was so misunderstood that efforts to assess the challenges associated with the transition of the legal system were quickly frustrated. The reason is that the old communist legal and social control mechanisms were built on an altogether unfamiliar premise for those accustomed to thinking about law and social control in developed Western-style systems: that laws should be as ambiguous as possible so that people are unclear about exactly what they can and cannot do. Under these conditions they shrink from testing the system because it has promised a harsh and arbitrary response. Western legal systems, in contrast, try to construct rules as specifically as possible; this approach, however, carries the added burden of implying that all behaviors not explicitly prohibited are legal. The most obvious benefits of the communist system for managing, controlling, or manipulating people were not apparent to the public but certainly must have been clear to those governing. It was efficient and effective.

All of the transitional states have committed themselves to creating new systems in which laws are specific, understandable, and applied in a nonarbitrary way. That means that they are developing legal frameworks similar to those found in liberal, democratic, developed political systems. The result for most Southeast Europeans will be that most will have more, not fewer, encounters with police and the government, as people probe the limits of the new and specific rules. More, not fewer, police will be needed to deal with the pressure from the public to find the new limits, especially in economic behavior. More court cases, attorneys, regulations, and visibility for legal considerations have already resulted. It is reasonable to assume that these conditions will generate negative feedback for the regimes. The new legal systems are dealing with public pressure and resentment that may articulate itself in challenges to incumbent leaders at the ballot box.

Corruption

Corruption may be another telling signal in the effort to understand how these countries are doing in the transition. Slovenia and Bulgaria perform reasonably on this measure. Campaigns to reduce corruption in Romania have been ineffective. The unrated countries should be understood to be so deficient in data and performance as to be neglected by the researchers for the World Economic Forum. They include Macedonia, Bosnia, Serbia/Montenegro, and Albania. Table 6 (chapter 8) summarizes these findings.

Corruption is the systemic equivalent of cancer. It represents truly malformed behaviors by select actors in the political system, most often for personal financial gain. The cost to the system is much greater than the simple concentration of financial resources that can result. Worse is the corrosive effect on public attitudes and commitment to government both within and outside bureaucracies. Corruption is often illegal behavior but it can also be genres of behavior that have not yet been added to the legal prohibitions of the system. In this context, the maneuvering is often *gray-area behavior* that violates the intent of the law but not the letter of the law.

This dimension of a political system is a constant focus for evaluation. In the special context of Southeast Europe, the EU has worked persistently to model behavior and administrative mechanics to address the phenomenon. The proportions and pervasiveness of the problem may reflect a number of threads from the socialist past. Low-level "appropriating" of workplace materials was rationalized by the notion that all such things were socially owned and one "needed" x or y. "To each according to his needs" was a major precept. Pay was meager and sometimes unreliable. Some reasoned that socialism in reality was man against the system and workplace theft was one of the options for "fighting back." Socialism in its practical application often contorted morality when it came to property. Beyond that, the "new" capitalist system touts the "freedom" to do whatever is not proscribed by law. It charges: do all you can do to further your own financial and personal well-being. Think first of one's self and others will do the same. Buoyed by such rationalizations and faced with systemic confusion, many insiders and inventive types seized the window of opportunity and made fortunes from nothing but their comfort with risk and initiative. The situation has been labeled an endemic culture of graft.

More than any other factor, corruption challenges the system—challenges the very rules of the system. From the public's view, those that show least respect for the rules, gain the most. The result can be chronic, terminal decline. Remedies exist that, while imperfect, have the ability to check the spread of the disease. As with medicine, long experience is the source of viable solutions. Attempts to reinvent the wheel—that is, design from scratch a country-unique response to such corrupt behaviors—underestimate the flexibility of the challenger and may prove frustrating, ineffective, or worse. Moises Naim's new book *Illicit: How Smugglers, Traffickers, and Copycats are Hijacking the Global Economy* (New York: Anchor, 2006) is a fascinating testimony to the stealth and capacity of organized crime and shadowy organizations.

Southeast Europe is one of those regions that must face the challenge squarely. The progress toward democratic development can be short-circuited by high and refined levels of corruption. The EU has devoted both guidance and money to assist new members and candidate member states with the arduous process of screening out corruption. Predictably, resistance comes from those who have something to lose. In the halls of government, the arguments may be technical and narrow-gauge but the reality of corruption persists. Reforms targeted at corruption threaten a particular elite in the interest of the broader society. Tactics that bury or neutralize anticorruption efforts are legion and can be found in virtually every system in Southeast Europe. As noted above, studies have identified a few Southeast European states that have accepted the wisdom and embraced the costs of confronting corruption. Slovenia and Bulgaria followed by Croatia have made significant progress. But most of the states remain mired in shortsighted and self-interested debates with no results. The absence of armed conflict certainly enables a political system to direct itself, if the will exists, to addressing corruption.

One such example is rather surprising under the circumstances. In late 2006, Romania was facing an imminent decision by the EU regarding its membership date. Postponement was an option; key was the Romanians' commitment to moving deliberately against systemic corruption. Surprisingly, in mid-autumn 2006, the Romanian legislature took a decision to back away from a policy that would have underlined and reinforced the government's anticorruption efforts. The specific law would have empowered the Romanian special prosecutor for corruption cases to investigate and indict senior politicians and judges. The special prosecutor had been active but unable to pursue cases near the top of the system. In 2005, records revealed 451 indictments for corruption, with 170 of those convicted. But none were key or ranking officials. With the advent of an executive decree in September 2005, the office began investigations on three prominent Romanian officials. When time came for the legislature to make the decree permanent, the effort failed. Conventional wisdom in Romania speculates that persons of privilege were able to thwart the legislation and, in so doing, remain out of the reach of the law. Of course it may be that the investigation of the three highly visible Romanians was enough to persuade the EU that Romania is genuine about addressing the problem. The three include a former prime minister, Adrian Năstase (currently speaker of the House of Parliament); political party leader Dan Ioan Popescu; and George Copos, a Romanian tycoon. All claim that the investigations are politically motivated.

Efforts toward an independent judiciary have been set back by this decision even though political rhetoric acknowledges the necessity of both EU membership and democratic development. Unfortunately, the EU has already established a pattern of ignoring some of its own criteria when faced with accession decisions. It once again looked past this counterreform decision and left Romanian on the calendar for January 1, 2007 membership. Nonetheless, the recent Romanian decision reflects an absence of political will to fight the necessary fight against corruption in high places. The centrist government currently in power is acutely aware that Romania's political culture has been characteristically plagued by corruption made all the worse by "mushrooming" trends since the collapse of communism. While the EU is a consideration, the strongest motive for attacking corruption is the benefit such a move would bring to the Romanian public.

Serbia has also acknowledged that it has a persistent problem with corruption. The Milošević administration was especially insulated from scrutiny and many of the elements of that regime remain central players in Belgrade. In fact, Milošević's Socialist Party (even with his persona removed) is a part of the ruling coalition. The Koštunica government has chosen to pursue criminal charges against one of its tycoons turned politician, Bogoljub Karic—a key partner with the government (Post, Telegraph, and Telephone) in the mobile telephone business in Serbia (Mobtel). Karić's company BK Trade is actually the partner and it controls the systemwide TV channel BK TV. Speculation rages in Serbia over whether Karić went into politics because he saw the investigation looming or whether he is a target because he went into politics. Granted, he has entered the political arena in a very controversial way. His fledgling Power of Serbia Movement (read: political party known as PSS [Socialist Party of Serbia]) is undermining the coalition under Koštunica by poaching MPs from the government coalition. Such poaching is possible because MPs in Serbia are the "owners" of their parliamentary seats; parties do not have claim to the seats. Thus when an MP changes parties, there is nothing that can be done from the establishment's perspective. In effect, the Serbian system is premised on the notion that elected MPs are "trustees" in the eyes of the system; that is, once elected it is their *own* judgment that matters, not that of their constituents or the position of their political party. The threat to the stability of the Koštunica government is perceived to be grave enough to change the law to prescribe that seats are the domain of the political parties and cannot be converted to another affiliation without a new election.

The current majority in Belgrade is so thin that such poaching renders a real threat to the survivability and control of the leadership. The stark possibility that Karić could seal a vote of no confidence in the parliament is reason alone to be wary. Throughout the postcommunist systems of Central and East Europe, tycoons seem to run into focused legal scrutiny as soon as they develop political aspirations. Add the ownership of media (common among tycoons) and one has a spotlight cast on his activities. Usually the record is gray enough and the tax reporting spotty enough to bring prosecution. The Russian experience is the one most publicized but many examples can be uncovered. In Karić's case, he clearly had the support of the government as he maneuvered to achieve his fortune. It was the government that chose to partner with him and the government who issued him the license to broadcast throughout Serbia. Karić's relationship with Milošević cooled but not enough for the reform government under Djindjić, who saw Karić as a highly visible target. Various efforts to investigate were unproductive until Karić in 2004 inaugurated his own political party. In that presidential election Karić finished third. He was buoyed by consistently positive coverage and regular coverage by his own BK TV. Karić's party is a significant player, often outpolling the major parties including the ruling party. One Serbian political observer describes Karić as "a kind of populist that tends to flourish in countries like Serbia which are undergoing traumatic economic transition."[1] Others use the term *demagogue*. His party campaigns without a lucid political program. It is simply the party of Karić. His 13 percent of the vote is significant in the party-laden multiparty system of Serbia. He also has played to the beleaguered Serbian population in Kosovo.

Serbia's government actor in this case is the Council Against Corruption. The actual details of the case are too entangled to sort out here. The politically salient point is that governments in Southeast Europe have a very hard time investigating and prosecuting leadership elites because of the lose-lose scenario for government. If they pursue those most likely to have engaged in corruption—especially top politicians—they will be criticized for attacking political opponents. If they ignore the transgressions, they will be criticized for harboring and abetting corrupt elements. All said, effective prosecutions are very low among significant players in the political and business environments in the region. Some believe that the best-case scenario is one in which the government sends a message by attempting to prosecute a tycoon and having others, as a result, reduce their gray-area operations and enhance their activity in the legal economy.

Civilian Control of Military

Constraint is also required if a political system is to retain control of all the coercive forces in society. Reality dictates that societies will have some sort of military establishment. By its nature, the military can challenge or thwart political authority unless it is constrained by both *self-imposed* boundaries of political engagement and by formal political measures that maintain civilian control. If the military is directed by elements not under the authority of the civilian government, it is impossible to claim that the system is democratic. Southeast Europe of late has not been prone to military regimes but it has numerous cases of military groups operating independently or with large measures of autonomy from the central governments. In such cases, claims about democratic development are problematic at best.

Indeed constraint and transparency challenge the structure and behavior of every military in Southeast Europe. The recent "velvet divorce" between Serbia and Montenegro will challenge both new states to embrace democracy-supporting modes of organization and behavior. As a joint force (the Yugoslav army), they were not effectively brought under civilian control. Without affirmative guidance from the top, each will continue to witness financial and political abuses. Watchdog elements in either country are unwilling and unable to perform adequately. Reforms have lost all momentum in Serbia, even with NATO encouragement or in reaction to it. The Serbian military under Milošević was less central to political control than was the Serbian police, Milošević's favorite instrument of power. Military professionalism and capabilities suffered under the former regime. When NATO attacked Serbia in 1999, the military enjoyed a new honeymoon that proved essentially political. Its military efforts were feeble and impotent. It was ill-prepared and ill-equipped for its contest with NATO.

When the coalition of political forces (Democratic Opposition of Serbia) managed the removal of Milošević, the military lurked in the shadows in an effort to avoid its own renewal. It succeeded. But the Djindjić government eventually got around to purging the military of wanted war criminals and other tainted military leaders. Under a new aggressive defense minister, Boris Tadić, reforms were begun. By 2004, downsizing and streamlining was beginning with both tactical and technical changes settling in. The primary emphasis has been on ensuring civilian oversight and routinizing accountability to civilian authorities. The defense ministry and the parliament were given roles, especially in oversight of intelligence activities. The effort was not without formidable efforts to dilute the changes. The resistance continues. And Djindjić, a strong proponent, was assassinated.

"Checks and Balances" in Design

Constraint on the systemic scale is frequently built in by way of so-called checks and balances. Clearly, these reflect an effort to constrain the exercise of power by distributing power and by forcing a measure of collaboration that requires compromise or mediation. By distributing levers of power, the system constrains the singular exercise of authority by necessitating contact with and gestures toward other functional elements of the system. In its most lucid form, a system designates concrete procedures for the creation of or implementation of policies.

Legislative-Executive Relations

The first specific challenge of redesign was how to delineate and institutionalize the relationship between the legislative and executive branches of government. The design of these two components literally defines a democracy, in that it guards channels of input for public views and creates boundaries for the use of authority by those two key actors. Unfortunately, designing the relationship is just half the battle. It is as essential that the design process generates a genuine appreciation for, and commitment to, behaving according to the design. The subtle point here is that the respect of each part for the role and responsibility of the other is as important as the structural design itself. One way to achieve that mutual respect is to make the design process and the logic that underpins it as transparent and publicly accessible as possible. In this way suspicion, distrust, and skepticism can be minimized.

Slovenia and Bosnia, for different reasons and in different ways, neglected to wrestle with this challenge. Slovenia quickly created a parliamentary system. Parliamentary systems ask the public to elect legislators who, based on the levels of electoral party support they received, elect one of their own to serve as the executive. In this crucial sense, the executive-legislative relationship is inherently established with a high level of transparency and routine. The Bosnian case stands in sharp contrast to the Slovenian experience. The international community imposed on Bosnia a system that nearly defies description. Its presidency consists of three individuals, none of whom is directly elected by all the people. If any of the ethnically elected parties is judged to be unacceptable to the U.N. high representative, that elected official can and has been replaced. The political system has two legislatures that function spasmodically. Technically, one is the legislature for the Srpska Republic of Bosnia and the other is the legislature for the Federation of Croats and Muslims of Bosnia. They do not coordinate policy decisions. Worse, the protracted negotiations to produce a constitution for Bosnia to replace the Dayton Accords failed to generate the compromises that would allow for any results.

Economics

Emerging markets are societies that have been committed by leaders or circumstance to developing economic markets in an environment characterized by private ownership, profit motivation, relatively free prices, and a fluid labor market. As the term also implies, these economies are understood not to have reached that goal. In fact, they are judged to be in the early phases of the journey. They typically experience high rates of growth and dramatic fluctuations in their economies, all of which are reflected in economic data. Because of that fluctuation it may be misleading to provide economic figures for a single slice of time. Regionally, annual growth rates average around 4.5 percent. Deficits are higher than they were a decade ago, and some argue that the costs associated with accession to the EU are the reason. In most of the countries, economic prospects are buoyed by optimism, but unemployment and declining foreign direct investment remain worrisome.

The postcommunist transition will require a long inventory of economic changes, among them the following:

- Establishing a consumer logic to serve as a platform for consumer behavior that conforms to market concepts. Price (or cost) sensitivity to basic purchase decisions is key.
- Establishing a link between worker productivity and wages.
- Establishing a consumer and commercial credit system in which people (and especially entrepreneurs) embrace risk for the goal of long-term business performance and success.
- Establishing a basic understanding of competitiveness, especially in an international market environment.
- Establishing an investment and savings mentality that could nourish and sustain investment.
- Reconceptualizing the role of government to other than that of sole provider of essential services and living conditions.
- Establishing a philanthropic mode of behavior that could ease pressure on government to provide all services.

As one can readily see, these are changes in *culture*—changes that refocus public thinking and behavior in postcommunist societies. It should be clear as well that these changes are hard to measure. Different countries responding to different leadership will display very different levels of success. Even in places where efforts have been focused on the points in the above list, scholars understand that it will take time to transform thinking. In a sense, the acceleration of thinking and behavior in Southeast Europe has been remarkable. These changes are key to how the political system will unfold.

Chapter 6

Transparency

The people out there in America know that life is not as simple as what they see on the news: a world of heroes and villains, winners and losers, exploiters and victims. Yet that's how we show them night after night.
—Andrew Heyward, president, CBS News

The most significant development that accelerated the search for common values was the emergence of the European Union. By 1992, just as communism was disintegrating in the region, Western Europe was raising its level of integration from the European "Community" to the European "Union." In essence, the relationships in that region were made more binding, involving some sacrifice of political sovereignty by member states. As postcommunist political systems in the region began foundering, the European Union provided an elaborated set of societal goals and an organizational "destination" for these countries that were best captured in the requisites for formal membership. It should be added that these conditions are negotiable and flexible, open to sundry interpretations and situations:

- A stable system of democratic government
- Institutions that ensure the rule of law and respect for human rights
- A functioning and competitive market economy
- An administration capable of implementing EU laws and policies

These conditions set the destination for all aspiring member societies—past, present, and future.

Institutional Limits

Transparency in decision-making is requisite to democratic development. It would be naïve, however, to ignore the fact that transparency brings with it many incumbent costs to those in power. The public, or elements of it, may be motivated by other than system-supporting interests. The specter of transparency may prevent capable leaders and administrators from accepting roles in the political system. In extreme cases, transparency is revealed to have no natural boundaries; in such environments, many personal and private elements of one's life are exposed. Transparency can also change the nature of the dialogue that predates policymaking or the policymaking process itself. This change can and does make the candid and penetrating discussion of policy nearly impossible. In an evolving democratic environment, none of these drawbacks cancel out the need for transparency. Nevertheless they do remind us that democratic systems will likely seek out design features that curb wanton and unrestricted probing. This process of "seeing" what goes on in government must fall to both internal and external players in the system. Democratic governments need "watchdog"-style assessors with powers both within a bureaucracy and across bureaucracies and other component parts of the political system. Where these assessors are slow or hesitant to scrutinize, only the independent press and academic professionals have the resources and explicit responsibility to examine and evaluate the system. Apart from all these considerations, issues of state security—given the nature and perception of threats and the requirements associated with responses to them—raise delicate issues in a democracy.

Accountability and Reports to the Masses

One rather effective method for backgrounding the public in the affairs of state—and thereby enlisting them in the governing process—is to issue credible, periodic, and targeted reports on what government is doing. CEOs find it necessary and useful to do this in the corporate setting (especially to stockholders) and governments would do well to make such effort with stakeholders (broadly defined) as the consumers. Democracies struggle with this reporting because of the reticence of regimes to give quarter to their critics. Nonetheless, insightful regimes will understand that it is far better for them to assess their performance than to permit the opposition the monopoly on such critiques. Parliamentary systems are much better at embracing this reality than are presidential systems. When elite assessments are made of an issue ("white papers," commission reports, special investigations, and so forth), rendering these in readable form and length for public consumption is crucial to the creation of confidence and patience necessary in transitional and aspiring democratic systems.

It is important at this point to remember that in a democracy all elements of the system are accountable—not only the elites. One of the dynamics that make democracies so hard to establish and maintain is that the public, its many agents and would-be agents, as well as the myriad organizations that frame issues in society *all* have responsibility and accountability. All the players in the system must be subjected to measures of accuracy and integrity. If the public plays by different rules, the elite have little chance to establish effective leadership. The primary "source" of this accountability must be the public itself. The people must diligently scrutinize the things said in their name and accept the consequences if misrepresented; that is, they must embrace their own accountability. Accountability, in a very real sense, must predate transparency. Transparency is the lens through which the elements of the system—both the elite and the masses—can see the accountability process.

While many examples of attempts to forge accountability in Southeast Europe are at hand, perhaps none are more tangled than those emanating from Kosovo. Accountability in an environment in which a sovereign state is disintegrating is especially messy. A large and organized effort by what represents itself as an official Kosovar government delegation has made a full-scale assault on the Serbian government for compensation owing to action taken by the former "Yugoslav" government, which at the time was the legitimate political authority in Kosovo. The particulars include (1) lost income and pensions to Kosovars resulting from anti-Albanian discrimination, (2) war damage to property, (3) foreign debt (embraced under Serbian authority), and (4) costs associated with creating a successor state. The position taken suggests that Belgrade owes Pristina many hundreds of millions of euros.[1] The claim is that Belgrade is responsible for nearly €900 million in debt incurred in the name of Kosovo but resulting from Belgrade's policy decisions.

The broader claim involves the full range of elites in Kosovo. It is a desperate effort to prime an economic pump that is bone-dry. Serbian liability is very problematic. Nonetheless, the effort is elaborately organized. Eight working groups, thirty delegates, and economic "experts" frame the Kosovar claim. Among the most interesting features of the effort is a report purporting to assess Kosovo's "overall economic sustainability." That document, when made public, should be of very special interest. It is likely to concede the tenuous economic platform for the new Kosovar state.[2] The future, tiny, landlocked country will have to deal with the question of its long-term economic viability. Production of competitive products is close to zero. Exports have declined sharply from very small in 2004 to negligible in 2006. Mushrooms represented the major export product in 2005. Unofficial United Nations Mission in Kosovo (UNMIK) sources anticipate a "looming disaster" for the fledgling economy.

The economic performance figures are open to active debate as international agencies are likely to revisit Kosovo's fiscal obligations when the province becomes an independent state. The Badinter Commission of the EU more than fifteen years ago rejected Kosovo's claim to be an equal constituent part of former socialist Yugoslavia; Kosovo was thereby not entitled to make claims of assets and liabilities. The current claim must challenge this finding, establishing instead that Kosovo *did* contribute to former socialist Yugoslavia in ways comparable to those of the former republics. Only in this way can Kosovo hope to recover at least the bank assets that were kept in Belgrade. Pristina has demanded €300 million in pension funds, €150 million deposited in Kosovo accounts in Serbian banks, and millions more to compensate for war damage. Claims are made all the more complicated by the concept of "socially owned property"—the standard premise in socialist Yugoslavia.

Elite Accountability and Elite-Mass Interface

Legitimacy by results implies a strong measure of elite accountability. Many scholars focus on elite accountability when thinking about the meaning of democracy. A more fundamental balance that must be struck in any democratic or aspiring democratic system is between elites shaping public opinion and elites responding to public opinion. It is not helpful to be too simplistic about this dimension. Clearly, both dynamics exist; the balance can change from moment to moment and certainly from administration to administration. If a pattern exists in Southeast Europe, it would seem to be that leaders subscribe intellectually to the notion that they should be responsive both to situations and to public opinion. Their political gut, however, warns them to be skeptical of the "wisdom of the majority," who indeed are unfamiliar with civil society and participatory politics. The problem is exacerbated by the absence during the communist period of political and civic education that would motivate and energize the public to engage themselves in civic affairs.

Transparency receives a great deal of lip service in Southeast European politics; indeed, it is pivotal for EU qualification. Nonetheless, little has been attempted and still less has been achieved in firmly establishing transparency as a valued *elite goal.* The tendency has been to see public scrutiny as an impediment to efficient governing—something that delays and muddies the policymaking process. That perception, of course, is well known in established democratic systems. In Southeast European politics, transparency is understood largely as requisite for effective opposition party politics rather than as generic advantage for the public's understanding of political processes. Whichever master it serves, in those political systems outside the realm of EU politics, transparency will be one of those variables that can only gestate slowly and likely with fits and starts, advances and reversals. In contrast, EU member states will have little choice but to conform to the rigors and norms of political experience with transparency.

No process more clearly begs for transparency than the privatization of former state assets (socially owned assets). The missteps in the transition of socially owned assets since the demise of the communist system have characterized both mismanagement of leadership and the negative response of the public to the transition. The Kosovo Trust Agency (KTA) is an example of international efforts to open the process to public exposure and critical scrutiny. This agency, established by UNMIK (June 2002), has created a process that opens itself to monitoring and protects public revenues that result from its efforts. The environment in which it was created could not have been more dire. At the end of 1999, Kosovo's economy was virtually nonexistent. It had been destroyed by war but underfinanced and mismanaged for years before that. Kosovo was incapable of producing (and certainly far from ever producing) anything on a competitive level. The international community, once involved in Kosovo, discovered just how imposing the challenge would be to get Kosovo, not back on its economic feet, but for the *first time* on its feet! Privatization was the vehicle but both publicly owned (infrastructure enterprises) and socially owned enterprises needed this attention. The KTA had the distinct advantage of having been created by a Western authority, not a local government that might have political debts to repay. The KTA had ultimate power to reorganize using proven corporate models and corporate "best practices." Records, training, reporting, recruiting, corporate governance, executive accountability—all became part of the KTAs efforts as firms were prepared for privatization. In many respects even more important was the requirement that proceeds from all sales be held "in trust." Some firms were divided to rationalize their business activities. The KTA has come to manage 90 percent of Kosovo's industrial base, 20 percent of its agricultural assets and 60 percent of its forests.[3] KTA's successes are real (and impressive) but they represent a small fraction of the six hundred–plus firms that are on the block scheduled for privatization. The good news is that the Kosovo privatizations to date have met the test of transparency. They have been open and accessible to scrutiny from the media and the public. The bulk of such transactions in the region have not met those standards.

This brings us to elite-mass interface: the dynamic between the governed and those governing. For Southeast Europeans and many others, this discussion begins and ends with elections. This notion is particularly dangerous: it leaves the rather tenacious impression that democracy is simply about choosing a leader. If the relationship stops there, it is impossible to claim that a democratic process exists. Emerging from the legacy of the socialist period, a large number of Southeast European elites perceive that once they are elected, they have an electoral mandate to rule as a supertrustee (some would argue, king). In other words, their democratic responsibilities are diminished, set aside, or minimally subject to singular interpretation by the elected leader. In fact, democracy requires an ongoing relationship that is bi-directional and tempered by a common awareness that the leaders are stewards and the public must opt to be engaged. Opting out leaves the elites with no partner, no counterpoint, no sounding board.

Budgeting, Committees, and Independent Think Tanks

There may not be a governmental function that is of so much general concern as budgeting. (Nor may there be one about which so little is understood). Political systems are always challenged by the task of generating revenue, making tough choices about allocations, and then ensuring that the plan is executed within margins. If that process ever seems to move closer to completion (and it seldom does), the process in fact has begun again in yet another "backroom." For a democracy, publishing the budget is not transparency. For the public, even the educated public, to know anything useful about the budget, it must first and foremost "see" the process of shaping the budget. We know various parts of government make requests but we need to see the process by which those allocations decisions are actually made. We need to know by what criteria each was placed in the "needs hierarchy." For most persons living in aspiring democratic systems, such as those in Southeast Europe, understanding where and on what rationale monies are being allocated can engender confidence, nurture patience, and reinforce legitimacy. A lack of transparency can just as easily—perhaps more easily—erode public confidence in a system.

The design, composition, and activities of committees, whether legislative or executive is one of those elements that can contribute to confidence and legitimacy, especially early in the experience of a new democracy. By opening committee activities to public scrutiny and embracing the incumbent criticism that comes with it, new political systems can point to their commitment to transparency. As suggested earlier this commitment becomes an even greater asset when done—or a greater liability when *not* done—in the realms of budget, defense, and public welfare.

Committees in political systems with new structure, new architecture, can serve to deepen the background and expertise of legislators. At the same time, they may narrow the expertise of the legislator. In the socialist system, it was common for legislative committees either not to exist at all or to serve in very perfunctory ways. This virtual nonexistence minimized the ability of legislators to critique, modify, or find sound basis for rejecting legislative proposals emanating from the executive. The creation of so-called standing committees regularizes the focus of member legislators and enhances the policy process (though often delaying it at the same time). Committees also tend to create an intermediate leadership group by the roles and platforms given to a larger circle of legislators.

The deliberations of a committee can be another "window" on the policy process. Yet a delicate balance must be struck in a transitional system between providing muscle and visibility to committees and encouraging them to become singularly confrontational arenas or entities whose propensity would be to short-circuit the policy process simply because they can. Parliamentary systems are likely to display the sorts of party discipline that can "manage" these challenges more than presidential systems. The patterned role of committees may well serve as a sound indicator of political development and, given a focus on the considerations above, could well indicate the democratic tendencies of that development. Evidence of committee development is clear in Slovenia, beginning in Romania, Bulgaria and Croatia, and problematic in the remaining states (Serbia, Montenegro, Macedonia, Albania, Bosnia, and Kosovo).

Although we often think about transparency in terms of government opening and committing itself to transparency, for the infant system to establish itself on a firm democratic basis, other players need to embrace the concept as well. These others must do it independently; that is, without pressure or regulation from the government. In a noninstitutionalized setting, independent organizations and elements hoping to play a role in policymaking must set an example for society and the government by themselves modeling transparent behaviors. Without this, the public will grow weary and skeptical about the posture taken by think tanks and other such groups. If an NGO assumes a policy posture parallel to government's, it may be perceived as being in the pocket of government. If it takes issue with the government's position, the public may imagine a connection with the opposition. If a policy-focused and independent organization is to maintain its integrity in the minds of the public, it must be prepared to take transparency to a high level: revealing its sources, data, and framework for analysis. It must be prepared to embrace the highest standards of transparency especially surrounding relationships and financing.

Media Constraints and Media Sustainability

The place and latitude for operation of the media in a political system are central to the development of democracy. Tolerance, transparency, constraint, obligation, legitimacy, and voice are all commingled in and around the media in any society. One explicit consideration in the media derives from the ownership and/or control of the outlet. In Southeast Europe we find a variety of conditions and circumstances that influence the control of media outlets. Some outlets are state-owned and -operated. Others are owned by political parties and, as such, are linked inextricably with partisan interests and objectives—either regime or opposition. Still others are foreign-owned; they are generally considered organized, professional, politically neutral—and *suspicious.* A few examples of privately owned and operated media can also be found in the region. Even when ownership is not the central issue, the public seems prone to expect politically slanted and loaded reporting. Commonly, one will hear that it is essential to read a minimum of two newspapers to have any balance in one's news. Television is fast replacing newspapers as the public's primary source of information (such is also the case in the more developed democracies). Television is more encapsulated, is visually more interesting, and is free.

In those places where government media competes with private media, the sustainability of the private media is in doubt. Rather than seeing media pluralism as a strength for the democratizing process, regimes tend to see private sources of information as sinister, negative forces that would be better muzzled or dissolved. Governments have multiple levers of power for assaulting such outlets—including the very powerful weapon of taxation. Media outlets in classically small countries compete for advertising dollars and other support with a government that can and does allocate contracts, target businesses for investigation, and distribute honors and other rewards for loyalty. It is an uneven playing field at best. Many private outlets hang on the very thin thread of the quality of their writing and independence.

The 2006 developments in Montenegrin politics involving its departure from the union with Serbia presented a window on what many believe was an example of government efforts to shape the outcome of the all-important referendum. One specific case involved the dismissal of a program director on the principal state-run broadcaster, TV CG (Television Cerna Gora). The firing set off a mass resignation by the remaining editorial staff of the firm. It was widely believed that the problem stemmed from the measured support the station had provided for the independence effort. Reforms had just two years earlier transformed TV CG into a public service broadcaster, effectively establishing it as a more independent media outlet. Leadership of the station was now in the hands of those appointed by other than political leaders. Major political parties then maneuvered to extend their influence (and have been able even today to maintain much of their influence over editorial policy). At the same time, far more balance had been introduced into the station's political news—whether administration or opposition focused. The run-up to the referendum was contentious and early polls suggested a rather even split in public attitudes, heightening the stakes in the media. The station was demonstrating more and more independence through 2004–2005 on a variety of government proposals.

One watchdog media NGO wrote, "The editorial team of TV CG had been replaced because they were doing their job professionally, because they were defending public interests instead of personal monopolies. We have reason to believe that the reason for Jaukovic's replacement was political in nature, and that the majority of the council who replaced him, had political motives for doing so."[4] A Vijesti editorial written by its director Ivanovic concluded,

"Even shy hints of the national television [broadcaster] distancing itself from the centre of power were not something that the authorities could let pass or accept as a democratic step forward in Montenegro."[5] The essential point here is that politicians in the region have not yet transformed their thinking to a fundamental democratic process underpinned by tolerance, pluralism and transparency.

In practical terms, "sustainability" is a mix of variables, including professionalism, sufficient resources, effective financial management—all in an environment that appreciates the role that media can play in cementing a democratic direction for a political system. The research represented in figure 1 is among the most comprehensive and useful to date. It purports to measure sustainability for the media outlets in the systems under our scrutiny—and it paints a rather dismal picture. Croatia seems a bit better positioned to sustain its media. The International Research and Exchanges Board–sponsored study of media sustainability in Southeast Europe suggests that three factors contribute to this more positive picture. First is the "strength" of Croatian civil so-

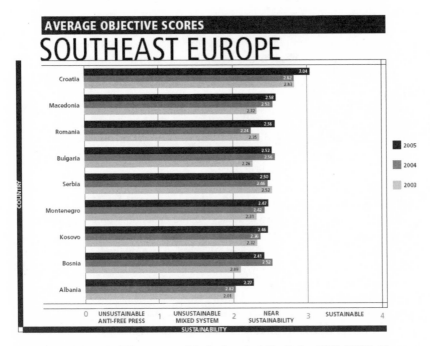

Fig 1. Media Sustainability. *Source:* Media Sustainability Index 2005, IREX, New York, http://www.irex.org/programs/MSI_EUR/2005/MSI05-SEEurope.pdf, p. 1. This report also includes detailed assessments of each of the systems examined in this volume.

ciety. Second is the "genuine political will" to adopt higher standards. Finally, they cite the strict EU monitoring associated with the path to membership. Collectively, these, according to the study, "make any open political pressure, harassment or direct political control over media almost unthinkable."[6] The trend reflected in Croatia is positive. The rest are in various and similar states of vulnerability, although only Bosnia and Bulgaria have displayed deterioration in their trajectories.

· · ·

To reiterate, transparency is crucial to the development of a democratic political system. No credible case can be made that meaningful participation is possible without the ability of the public, its agents, or the political opposition(s) to "see" the processes, responsible persons, or changes in the Establishment. As suggested earlier, for a democratic system to function, this transparency needs to penetrate to middle and lower levels as well. It must be embraced by those in government but also by those in organizations operating outside of government. Transparency is the foundation of public trust in or of public critique of the system.

Perhaps the most concrete, structural example of transparency in a political system is the routine built into many parliamentary systems owing their political heritage to the British. It is the so-called question hour, which can be any designated length of time set aside for the government—its ministers or prime minister—to answer virtually any question broached by the opposition. This mechanism is imperfect, and even in the routinized British system, it is often raucous and without a great deal of information flow. Nonetheless, it is a confirmed responsibility to provide the "others"—party or parties—with information in response to their probing. Whether by this means or another mechanism (say, the Freedom of Information Act), the principle that government cannot simply stonewall or entomb information that could illuminate problems or issues is at the heart of any new system.

Why is transparency so hard to achieve in the evolving systems in Southeast Europe? Certainly, the absence of commitment to this element in previous systems (especially the socialist systems that are the immediate predecessor of current political systems) is a factor. The disciplined study of political science was not part of the higher learning matrix in the former socialist systems, thus creating a conceptual void among some elites. Political inexperience of the leadership is another. There appears to be a reticence to embrace the notion that there is *any* upside for politicians to expose their efforts to broad public, journalistic, or academic scrutiny. Contributing to this sense is the clearly partial nature of what can be achieved and the presumption that impatience will lead to criticism, which will lead to nonsupport. This impulse is not unreasonable, given the skepticism and impatience that surface nearly everywhere polls are taken in the region. I would speculate (based upon a small number of professional conversations) that politicians do not understand that this reasoning sets in motion a vicious cycle: one that feeds skepticism and thereby sustains leadership resistance to transparency. A more subtle but real factor is the need for transparency to become a congruent and synchronous commitment from government and those being governed—most crucially from those organizations claiming to reflect the voice of the public and those either supporting or challenging the leadership. Without that commitment from civic society, the leadership can easily reason that the rules of the game are not uniform and disadvantage those playing by transparent behaviors. One must add to these lines of reasoning the more obvious: many leaders in the region have not yet embraced the commitment to what in this study has been called "obligation"; that is, the primary obligation to public interests. Thus pursuing personal interests and advantages become inevitable among "corrupt" officials who find transparency laughable.

The way out of this tangle of factors will require a system or two to mark the path and demonstrate that tangible political benefits accrue to the regime that embraces transparency. Progress can certainly be made incrementally as politically active elements in the broader society respond with their own behaviors. One could argue that Slovenia has already taken that step (largely at the prodding of the EU). Romania and Bulgaria will have to follow suit, although one should expect much slower progress in those cases. Croatia may also see the potential for a relationship with the EU. These changes will model behaviors that in time will cancel out some of the reasoning associated with resistance to transparency. Nonetheless, even with this positive scenario, those who guide political systems for their own gratification and enrichment (the "corrupt") will find cause to stifle reforms designed to enhance transparency.

Chapter 7

Legitimacy

To acquire immunity to eloquence is of the utmost importance to the citizens of a democracy.
—Bertrand Russell

Legitimacy is yet another basis for comparing and contrasting the Southeast European cases. Authority has many sources; some constitutional and routinized, others not. Legitimacy is a companion concept reflecting the sense among the governed that the person(s) with authority achieved that authority by established, proper means. In essence, leaders followed the rules and have power as a result. In this narrow sense, there is but one source of legitimacy—the people—and it is a fluid source as the people can readily change their views at any time.

Southeast European political systems obviously experienced the unsettling and abrupt collapse of the communist system. In this context, old and new elites scrambled to establish a grip on authority. Every political system went about creating new authorities, but very few understood enough about democratizing to make establishing *legitimacy* a priority. In the old communist system, legitimacy was presumed or ignored. Thus in the new political environment, many still believed it could be presumed. On reflection, this failing was predictable but unfortunate. Political scientists and public policy experts in even the most advanced of the Southeast European countries suggest that little time or effort was invested in building a foundation for legitimacy. The general comparative literature tells us that legitimacy can be built

- by procedure(s),
- by results,
- by habit,
- by identity.

We can surmise that most new political elites anticipated legitimacy by habit. Those leaders with an authoritarian bent tended to make this presumption. Those playing on ultranationalist themes nurtured legitimacy by identity (all Serbs support real Serbs). Those with greater focus on political development in the Western tradition began to work on legitimacy by procedures and results (we earn your trust). In general, the region was dismayingly feeble in its political maneuvers to establish legitimacy.

The Dead, the Dying, and the Difficult

The leadership conundrum in Southeast Europe is typical of many transitional and postcommunist systems. It is complicated by low levels of management experience (public or otherwise), thin circles of substantive expertise, fluid new institutions and elite conceptions of power and politics that are not yet "democratic." Sophistication about these things can be established only incrementally. It is unreasonable to expect instant refinement in the conduct and posturing of leadership—political, economic, social or religious—in political systems undergoing such profound transformation. It *is* reasonable, however, to identify those leaders and elite behaviors that slow or retard the movement toward "democracy" as we have defined it.

The record from the 1990s and the first decade of the new century reveals a number of political leaders who have missed or neglected opportunities to contribute to new patterns. Equally unsettling is the number of leaders who have died leaving untenable political situations. Djindjić, Serbian prime minister following the removal of Milošević from office, was assassinated; many attribute his murder to his effort to encroach on the gray economy and its profiteers. Rugova, the "father" of Kosovar independence and self-proclaimed president of Kosovo, died leaving a power vacuum. Milošević, often labeled the "black prince" of Balkan politics and former authoritarian leader of postsocialist Yugoslavia, has died while on trial in the Hague. Tudjman, "hero" of Croatian nationalism and authoritarian leader, died. Izetbegović, Bosniak nationalist largely responsible for complicating the Bosnian political environment to the point of rampant violence, is also dead. Trajkovski, Macedonian president and a reform-focused, young politician was killed in a plane crash. All shared an end that left the political environment with more problems than solutions. In the wake of such abrupt changes, transitional states face added legitimacy problems. Authoritarian leaders seldom groom successors; reformers often leave policies uncongealed and without strong advocacy. Legitimacy suffers also from the public's awareness of the ego-driven behavior of leadership.

Patterns of Leadership Turnover

The death of Kosovar President Ibrahim Rugova was a poignant case of impact-laden timing and serious political fallout. A power struggle has ensued in Kosovo's LDK party (Democratic League of Kosovo), the largest in Kosovo. The international community, still intimately entwined with the political management of Kosovo, is also scrambling. Rugova was not only president but also a cult hero of independence, an LDK leader, and the chief diplomatic negotiator in the delicate maneuver for Kosovo's independence.

Institutionally and technically, there appears to be a succession process. One would do well to acknowledge the problematic validity of the Kosovo "constitution." Nonetheless, it calls for the speaker of the parliament to assume the president's duties temporarily. That person was Nexhet Daci. The pivotal changes came just as negotiations on Kosovo's status was on the international agenda. Kosovo is managed as a protectorate of the U.N. But more than 90

Gandhi of the Balkans: President of a Phantom State

Ibrahim Rugova was born in a rural village in western Kosovo at the end of World War II. His father was executed by the new Socialist government of Yugoslavia. He pursued literary studies in France and was part of a small intellectual elite in Kosovo that formed in the 1960s and remained active for the next couple of decades. He was described as an enigmatic absent-minded professor, a casual "Left Bank"–looking intellectual with a trademark silk scarf around his neck and an ever-present cigarette. The year 1981 marked a watershed, when aggressive protest for "republic" status in socialist Yugoslavia was rejected. A resurgent Serbian nationalism pressed for Kosovo to be reintegrated as a part of Serbia. Rugova led the Kosovo Writers' Association and was spokesperson for resisting the Serbian initiative in the face of severe crimnial penalties. Rugova became a visible Kosovar leader, founding the Democratic League of Kosovo, advocating a passive resistance to Yugoslav control, and advocating for rights of Albanian Kosovars. He believed that a nonviolent strategy coupled with international support would ultimately prove successful. Two factors caused him to abandon this strategy: the formation of the KLA and the failure of negotiations at Rambouillet (1999). In March 2002 he was elected president of Kosovo.

percent of the population is of one ethnic identity and are pressing for independence from Serbia, while a significant Serbian minority resides in enclaves in Kosovo. Kosovo has for all modern times been a part of Serbia or its parent forms. Serbs, and a good deal of economic rationale, press Kosovo to remain a part of Serbia. Many saw the original negotiating team (membership established in September 2005) as the "A-team" of Kosovar leadership and the circle of potential successors. It initially included the then prime minister, Bajram Kosumi (Alliance for the Future of Kosovo); then speaker of the parliament, Nexhet Daci (LDK); opposition party leader, Veton Surroi (ORA); and former KLA (Kosovor Liberation Army) commander, Hashim Thaci (also an opposition party leader/Democratic Party of Kosovo). The effort to "balance" the team, however, resulted in disarray and division. None of them impressed the international community enough to establish an endorsement, formal or otherwise. Kosumi and Daci have already fallen from power (spring 2006). Without consistent leadership and stable, uniform positions, the Kosovo independence negotiation will find it difficult to establish and win its case. One prominent analyst claims: "Rugova's death has brought to the surface years of problems that have accumulated in Kosovar politics."[1] The search for new leadership is especially difficult because those popular in the Kosovo public's view (military leaders prominent among them) will not likely be the same as those seen as desirable based on the international agencies' priorities. Case in point: Agim Çeku has replaced Kosumi. His background with the KLA and later its successor, the Kosovo Protection Corps, gives the new government a decidedly military texture. His leadership is already under attack from his decision not to change key cabinet positions from the government of resigned Prime Minister Kosumi. It is argued that this retains the "politics of failure, mismanagement ad corruption." Crucially, the replacement Kosovar negotiating team includes Çeku (prime minister), Sejdui (president), Kole Berisha (speaker of the parliament), Hashim Thaci, Veton Surroi, and Blerim Shala representing opposition parties. The wistfully hopeful name of the new group is the "unity team."

Kosovo appears typical for the Southeast European region in terms of the types of leaders, established and aspiring, that are available. Daci is a chemistry professor in his early sixties with a reputation for being inflexible and whose commitment to democracy is suspect. Ironically, he was not supported by his most nationalistic peers in his own party and did not establish confidence among the international overseers in Kosovo. His resignation followed intraparty conflicts. Alush Gashi is a medical doctor in his late fifties who has nurtured support from the Kosovo diasporas in Europe and the United States. He is viewed as an effective parliamentary manager without much charisma.

Fatmir Sejdiu has the highest visibility within the LDK (ruling) party but is also viewed in neutral terms in the larger political system in spite of strong support from party rank and file. He eventually replaced Rugova as president and placed Çeku in the position of prime minister. Çeku has been labeled the most "trusted" public figure in Kosovo but is a man with singularly military credentials. He fought with the Croats against the Serbs in the early 1990s and led the KLA in 1999 against the Serbs. He formed the Kosovo Protection Corps out of the KLA to appease the U.N. Had the LDK been looking for young leadership with the prospect of long-term civilian control, Lutfi Haziri may have been the choice. In his late thirties, he is nonetheless a party veteran with more than fifteen years' experience in the party and a successful term as mayor of a Kosovar city.

Hashim Thaci and Ramush Haradinaj are also formidable players; both commanded the Kosovo Liberation Army and are generally recognized as "charismatic" leaders. Haradinaj had served briefly as prime minister but re-signed in March 2005 after being indicted by the War Crimes Tribunal in the Hague. Opponents of Çeku whisper that he too could be or should be indicted.

The so-called international community that genuinely manages Kosovo like a colonial entity (euphemism for "protectorate") has key players engaged in the political recruitment process. Søren Jessen-Petersen (head of the U.N. mission in Kosovo/UNMIK) and Martti Ahtisaari (U.N. convenor of talks on Kosovo's future) are most visible. They cannot be comfortable with the military texture of the current Kosovar "government." Many who have worked with the "international community" in Kosovo believe that the key focus of their concern is transparency in the new government.

Managing the pressures from business interests (so-called informal economic networks), entrepreneurs seeking special deals from privatization, and relatively inflexible feuds and hostilities in local settings are the most acute challenges facing any new leadership. At the time of this writing, talks on the status of Kosovo are stalled, largely owing to the fluid nature of Kosovo's leadership. Legitimacy will not be easy to establish under these circumstances.

The LDK cannot claim democratic legitimacy by example or by "results. It has itself avoided internal elections for party leadership for a decade and has resisted embracing democratic reforms in its own procedures. The LDK can hope that it will maintain some legitimacy by simple association with Rugova's name—a legitimacy by reflected glory. The negotiations with Serbia are critical: the outcome will define the path for Kosovo for generations. The leadership will bear the burden or bask in the glow depending on the result. The "unifying" figure that most seek in order for Kosovo to have a future is not clearly visible. Drift is possible and decline would certainly accompany it. Democracy will become a more distant objective. Once again the minority, this time the Serbian population in Kosovo, will suffer.

General "Comfort" Level with Leadership

Characteristically, Southeast European politics is high on expectations and modest on performance. Leaders tend to regale their achievements or imagined achievements to enlist support. Such a strategy is both typical of the former socialist system and can become volatile over time when public patience runs out. Many elements play into the texture of opinion regarding regime leadership. The bulk of these elements are critical and negative factors. We can turn to recent survey efforts in the region for more detail but before examining those data, let us consider the classic example of Albania. Albanians register serious reservations about their leadership as the high and unrealistic expectations about EU membership are confronted by the reality of very gradual progress toward the status required for membership. The unwillingness to reform policymaking and reinforce political institutions that can curb corruption, control organized crime, and create a stable environment for foreign investment have virtually halted the candidacy process. The EU is also cautious about the democratic routines built into elections and the transfer of power. The 2005 elections were a marked improvement but, for many observers, not yet a pattern. Pressure is building on the leadership given that polls suggest EU membership is the voters' highest priority. More than 80 percent report favoring prioritizing Albania's EU membership. The path, however, is full of steps that will call into question or dissolve much of elite privilege and unofficial profit opportunities. Reform is popular with the masses and threatening to the elite. Many, including many European diplomats, believe that Albanians have reached a consensus constructed around European values associated with democracy and meaningful definitions of human rights and market economy. In contrast, the elite understand (perhaps better than the public) that membership would obligate Albania to embrace laws, obligations, responsibilities, and behaviors that would both change and unsettle Albania. Britain's ambassador to Albania, Richard Jones, has articulated this reality most succinctly: "To put it bluntly, there will be winners and losers from the integration process and Albanians need to understand that clearly."[2] The result is likely to be a widening gulf between Albanian life and that of the Southeast European states moving more expeditiously toward membership. Concretely, visa-related mobility, investment-generated jobs and development, as well as in-bound tourism are sure to suffer for Albanians.

Still another example of a significant gap between policymakers and the masses is the example of Bosnia and the VAT (value added tax). On January 1, 2006, Bosnia imposed a flat sales tax (value added tax) of 17 percent on all items.[3] Although the last country in the region to do so, the postwar conditions compounded by unresolved issues of governmental design make the development especially painful. Desperate for cash flow to sustain the various governments in Bosnia, the decision was made and implemented. The U.N.'s high representative, effectively the governor of the country by default, has endorsed the policy as essential and argues that it moves Bosnia closer to serious consideration in the EU (though this claim is problematic). The struggling poor in Bosnia will be impacted dramatically. With little mobility and less income potential, they will see their living standards decline. The policy fails to differentiate staples from discretionary spending. It explicitly chose not to exempt flour, bread, oil, and milk or to place limits on profit margins of those commodities. Twenty percent of Bosnians officially live below the poverty level ($1000 annual income) and nearly 30 percent more are near that cutoff. In Bosnia nearly as many people are officially unemployed as the number officially employed (510,000 unemployed; 640,000 employed) in a country with roughly four million people in its total population. Both the Srpska Republic and the Federation (of Croats and Muslims) claim that they will respond with special aid programs for the most affected; many analysts believe, however, that once the money flows in, these governments will be temped to move in other directions. Others see the creation of a single policy for the entire country as a step toward rationalizing Bosnia as a political system—something quite hard to do as yet. Perhaps the most controversial claim is that the VAT will cause the black market in Bosnia to shrink. With conventional wisdom among observers in Bosnia estimating the black market represents roughly 30 percent of all economic activity in the country, it is hard to see how this shrinkage will result. It could cut in the opposite direction: many more Bosnians may engage in the gray market to avoid both paying the burdensome VAT and placing more money in the hands of an untrustworthy government. As the data that follow indicate, a disconnect between elites and masses in Bosnia is apparent. The public sees unemployment, public sector reform, and foreign trade deficits as major economic problems. The VAT addresses none of these, suggesting that the policymaking elites see the challenges differently. Bosnian stability is delicate at best, especially in light of the fact that it has not addressed financing "development." There is no monetary policy. Exchange rate policy is nonexistent. In essence, the instruments for managing the economy have not been created. Low growth and government deficits are the norm. The public recognize this; numerous polls indicate extraordinarily high rates of pessimism in Bosnia.

Still another case that demonstrates how challenging it is to establish legitimacy in transitional systems is the Democratic Party (DS) of Serbia. The party is the main centrist party in Serbia today. Its leader is Boris Tadic (also president of Serbia), by all accounts a very popular politician. Responding to internal conflicts and frictions, in 2006 the party changed its rules to "centralize" power around Tadic. The party's leadership is now voted on every four years instead of every two years. It also decided that the party leadership should be elected by the entire party membership but only after the current leadership leaves office—effectively exempting them from democratic and participatory input. The party's last leader, Zoran Djindjić, was assassinated in 2003 and that loss has left the party with organizational wounds. Clearly, the party is trying to insulate Tadic from internal challenges because of his broad public popularity (that, by association, accrues to the party). Roughly one-quarter of Serbs support Tadic and the Democratic Party (DS), making it a leading party, second only to the nationalist party, the Serbian Radical Party. The DS party changes are *democracy deferred* at best. A DS party activist is reported to have said, "There will be no democracy in society if there is no democracy within the Democratic Party, which is the backbone of democracy in Serbia. . . . Centralization has won out over democracy in our party."[4] The implication for legitimacy is clear.

Protest and Insurgency

These are the consequences of a political system losing legitimacy in varying degrees. Albania, Kosovo, and Bosnia exist in circumstances that invite behaviors associated with delegitimization. This is not to suggest that legitimacy problems are unknown in the other states: Croatia faces an Istrian independence challenge; Romania has the Transylvanian arena where pressures build periodically; Serbia has dealt with Montenegro and is about to wrestle with Kosovo in an international arena. Virtually every state has smaller regions pressing for concessions (and often more) from the central government. These demands are built upon a platform of rhetoric that calls the central authorities of the state into question by raising its own basis of legitimacy. Such latent forces in a state's politics can be minimized by diligent sensitivity to the public's sense of government legitimacy. If governments in Southeast Europe were more attuned to the multiple options for establishing legitimacy, they might well be able to curb dissident activity without coercive force.

Legitimacy is a political mechanism by which both mass and elite interests can be served in a healthy democratic environment. Once the public recognizes that they are the only source of legitimacy, they come to realize that they have a constant role to play in the system. Their collective judgment is the ultimate arbiter of procedures and those senses can be articulated either in protest or in the next sequence of elections if government is not meeting its obligations. Questions about legitimacy are the stimulus for healthy political dialogue and, if separated from more specific judgments about policy or short-term leadership popularity, can reinforce the important idea that one's approval or disapproval of a policy need not determine one's sense of legitimacy of a regime—and vice versa.

Legitimacy serves the government by this separation and makes possible policy initiatives that may be unpopular in the short run for various reasons. It is this difference that facilitates the banking of social capital in regimes. Legitimacy from the government's perspective is enabling in many ways. It can carry a regime over rough spots, downturns in performance, or through scandals. The attractiveness of building legitimacy is a function of the variety of means by which it can be created and banked. Because there is a range of tactics, all of which can be mixed and matched, every regime has options. Some strategies (that is, combinations of tactics) have long-term platforms; others, short-term. Recalling that legitimacy can be built by identity, procedures, habit, and results, a regime needs to be realistic and pragmatic about its credible options. Political systems in the region are sorely pressed to claim legitimacy by results save for those that have impressed the EU enough to be invited to membership. Legitimacy by procedures also requires time and public clarity of procedures. Habit is a very thin though sometimes essential basis. It is the quickest to erode when illuminated by an opposition. Legitimacy by association is a markedly dangerous and threatening basis: it has often been associated with strident nationalism and thus precludes minorities in a society from full participation. If framed as a patriotic appeal (that is, an identity with the political state), it can be more inclusive.

Perhaps most critical to this subject is the prospect that regime legitimacy can serve as an alternative to coercive force. If challenged by political forces that find the direction of policy or particular leadership unacceptable, a regime that has established its legitimacy can counter with political tactics. If it has not devoted sufficient effort in advance to nurturing legitimacy, it may find that it has no recourse but to use coercive force against its challengers. The good news for the region is that the EU brings with it refined techniques for eliciting legitimacy and the processes to sustain it. Regimes in the region are "learning" what can be accomplished politically by investing in the formation of legitimacy.

Chapter 8

Prescription for a Badly Scarred Body Politic

"Don't Happy, Be Worry"
—Rambo Amadeus

Prognoses are rather tricky things. Just as a doctor would want to factor in a patient's medical and personal history, we should want to be informed about the political heritage in Southeast Europe. And like the doctor, we then shall consider indicators present today in order to diagnose probable health tomorrow. Determining the prognosis is, in essence, the design of my short study. It examines the dynamics of politics in the region in the years since 2000 with an eye to the impact of those developments on tomorrow. Naturally there are inherent risks. Politics and societal life cycles change and morph in ways certain to make any prognosis imperfect. Nonetheless, the value of such an enterprise is clear: the prognosis then is the basis for the prescriptions.

In that vein, workable prescriptions for these transitional political systems are needed to compete with prescriptions generated by the leadership and experts in those countries. Prescriptions have the advantage of motivating specific behaviors and changes while never losing sight of the broader objective. Societal development sketched by and pursued by the very people who are being governed is one of those democratic goals. The earlier chapters have enumerated changes and behaviors that would create movement toward (or, in their absence, away from) democracy. It is essential to retain a realistic sense of what can be and how quickly it can be.

What Comparative Studies Tell Us

The World Bank study cited in chapter 1 examined 209 states in the world and assessed the efficacy of governance, comparing data from 1996 with 2004 (see table 5).[1] The authors claim that they have derived "workable measures of misrule" in this study. These measures presumably provide some sense of changes (direction and proportion) over that period. It is useful for us to have a comparative sense of those trajectories.

The data presented in this study signals caution for those anticipating democratic development in Southeast Europe. Slovenia fares very well on all six variables. The remaining political systems reflect the strain and challenges of the transition. On the voice and accountability factor, Serbia and Bosnia have yet to begin to manage constructively. Bulgaria and Romania have established positive patterns. Political stability has proven elusive for Albania, Bosnia, Macedonia, and Serbia. Only Croatia seems on a steady course. Government effectiveness and rule of law are the most problematic. Albania, Bosnia, Bulgaria, Macedonia, Romania, and Serbia fail to move their systems toward greater effectiveness, and rule of law is losing ground in virtually all systems, with Albania, Macedonia, Serbia, and Bosnia worst among the cases. As one would expect, the same systems also lose in their battle with corruption.

Drawing on the opportunity to use this data to generate perspective on where the regional states fit in the global pattern, Albania, Bosnia, and Kosovo are solidly mired around the lower third globally. Macedonia and Serbia find themselves just in the lower half of states while Croatia, Bulgaria, and Romania hover just above the mid-point, achieving upper half status. Slovenia ranks in the upper quarter of states, no doubt owing to its trajectory mentored by the EU.

Finally, by comparing the "net change" from 1996 to 2005 and the net change from 2004 to 2005, one can gauge whether new directions and efforts are creating positive traction. Most such comparisons do not yet suggest that this is happening. The essence of this data then is that improvements in government performance are uneven, modest, and spotty. Based upon this information, it is not possible to conclude that Southeast Europe is "slowly but surely" moving toward more sound governance. It is only clear that the pattern is erratic.

The World Economic Forum has also embarked upon the task of assessing the performance of governments, though with a more restricted scope. They examined four Southeast European countries in their sample of eighty countries, and Slovenia scored significantly higher than the other three that were proximate to one another. Significantly, the other states of the region (apart from Slovenia, Croatia, Romania, and Bulgaria) either chose not to submit data or were judged not ready for such scrutiny. This study focused on global competitiveness in general and three variables that gauge the effectiveness of "public institutions": (1) a government's capacity, (2) its record of controlling corruption, and (3) its effectiveness in establishing a sound legal system (see table 6).

TABLE 5
World Governance Study
Southeast Europe Directions of Change and Rankings, 2005 Scores

	Voice and Accountability				Political Stability				Government Effectiveness				Regulatory Quality				Rule of Law				Control of Corruption			
	Net change from '96	Net change from '04	Global %ile	Rank	Net change from '96	Net change from '04	Global %ile	Rank	Net change from '96	Net change from '04	Global %ile	Rank	Net change from '96	Net change from '04	Global %ile	Rank	Net change from '96	Net change from '04	Global %ile	Rank	Net change from '96	Net change from '04	Global %ile	Rank
Albania	−0.94		+0.08	49.8	−4.42		−0.68	27.4	−2.51		−0.49	35.9	−2.09		−0.27	45.0	−5.13		−0.84	21.3	−4.74		−0.76	27.6
Bosnia	−3.72		−0.11	43.5	−5.16		−0.78	24.5	−4.06		−0.53	33.5	−6.98		−0.53	31.7	−5.81		−0.74	30.4	−2.98		−0.32	46.3
Bulgaria	+3.25		+0.59	65.7	+0.08		+0.16	50.9	−2.09		+0.23	62.2	+2.18		+0.63	69.3	−1.07		−0.19	48.8	−1.83		−0.05	55.2
Croatia	+0.67		+0.51	61.4	+1.74		+0.32	58.0	+0.86		+0.44	67.5	+1.13		+0.45	65.3	−0.72		+0.00	53.6	−1.00		+0.07	59.1
Kosovo	N/A		−0.46	33.3	N/A		N/A	N/A	N/A		−0.76	26.8	N/A		N/A	N/A	N/A		−0.95	17.9	N/A		−0.67	32.0
Macedonia	−0.50		+0.03	48.3	−4.78		−1.04	19.3	−2.39		−0.28	47.4	−0.99		−0.20	48.5	−3.00		−0.38	43.5	−4.48		−0.50	40.4
Romania	+1.69		+0.36	56.5	+0.43		+0.03	46.2	−2.80		−0.03	56.9	+0.18		+0.17	58.4	−1.98		−0.29	45.4	−2.28		−0.23	51.7
Serbia*	−3.46		+0.12	50.2	−8.36		−0.91	20.8	−4.16		−0.31	45.5	−6.60		−0.53	32.2	−7.55		−0.81	24.6	−5.56		−0.55	39.4
Slovenia	+5.08		+1.08	84.5	+5.15		+0.94	80.7	+5.80		+0.99	78.5	+4.30		+0.86	74.8	+5.71		+0.79	74.4	+6.74		+0.88	80.3

*Montenegro is statistically included in Serbia given union.
"Scores" represent estimates ranging from −2.5 to +2.5.
"Rankings" are global percentile rank specified from 0 to 100.
Data drawn from: http://info.worldbank.org/governance/kkz2005/country_report.asp?

TABLE 6
Global Competitiveness and Political Effectiveness

	Global Competitiveness			Effectiveness Against Corruption	Effectiveness of Law
	2003	2005	2006	2006	2003
Slovenia	28th/80	30th/125	33rd/125	26th/80	26th/80
Croatia	58th/80	64th/125	51st/125	45th/80	60th/80
Bulgaria	62nd/80	61st/125	72nd/125	27th/80	67th/80
Romania	66th/80	67th/125	68th/125	67th/80	65th/80
Macedonia		75th/125	80th/125		
Serbia/Montenegro		85th/125	87th/125		
Bosnia/Herzegovina		88th/125	89th/125		
Albania		100th/125	98th/125		

Source: Drawn from world data set: Global Competitiveness, http://www.weforum.org/pdf/ Global_Competitiveness Reports/Reports/gcr_2006/gcr2006_rankings.pdf.

These data place Slovenia in a glowing spotlight. As suggested earlier, Slovenia has a number of advantages but is primarily reflecting the support and guidance provided by their very early entry (2004) into the EU. Bulgaria and Romania have just become members and Croatia is negotiating and approaching a timetable for accession. The study demonstrates clearly that these states are further along the path to making their economies sound and their political systems democratic. The omission of the other regional states by the World Economic Forum is itself a significant indicator.

Yet another intriguing study sponsored by the Fund for Peace and the Carnegie Endowment for International Peace examines 148 countries each year and assesses the degree to which they are "failing" in the performance of their mandates to govern (see table 7). While not specifically measuring democracy, the twelve indicators used reflect many of the prescriptions outlined in this book. The 2006 ranking of the states of Southeast Europe place Bosnia in the "in danger" category, the thirty-fifth worst-performing government in the world. Kosovo, were it included as a state, would most certainly rank worse still. The "borderline" category includes all the other countries of the region (except Slovenia which is placed in the "stable" category). The borderliners vary significantly. Consistent with the assessments from the World Economic Forum, the composite numbers suggest that Romania, Bulgaria, and Croatia are closest to improving their status. Serbia is significantly worse off than Macedonia which, in turn, is worse off than Albania. Only Serbia's situation deteriorated significantly from 2005 to 2006.

This data set illuminates a number of interesting notions. While the composite numbers suggest that Croatia, Bulgaria, and Romania are remarkably similar in their standing, it gives us the ability to see how different they are in terms of how they are approaching policy choices and strategies. For example, Bulgaria scores much worse than the other two in managing the military, avoiding sharp economic decline, and managing group grievances. Croatia performs much better on human rights and establishing legitimacy but struggles with refugee problems. Of the three, Romania is credited with best managing the security apparatus and is second only to Slovenia in the entire inventory. Bosnia, the "failed state" poster child in the region (until Kosovo is added) suffers most from refugee challenges, group violence, factionalized elites, and control by external actors. Serbia reflects a nearly identical pattern of performance problems, although in smaller measure. The study points to Macedonian problems with group violence and uneven economic development. Albania's challenges are with emigration, economic decline, and legitimacy.

Such comparative studies are very helpful, especially when they provide data over time. They make possible the refinement of prescriptions that "fit" the particular problems and adjust to the accomplishments of individual Southeast European states.

What This Study Tells Us

A brief look at the region's history suggests that there are elements of that past that can herald the development of democracy in Southeast Europe. These are mere threads of political and economic design but they could be woven into a new fabric. In essence, history can provide ideas and experiences useful to the creation of a modern, democratic system. Cited examples include tolerance, pragmatism, economic development as a platform for a system, potential roles for women, reliance on technocrats, precedent for wealth supporting legitimacy, and federalism. Many of these are found in Southeast European history, labeled otherwise or submerged among nondemocratic elements, but they were real and can be useful. The communist legacy leaves greater problems. Perhaps the toughest legacy to overcome is the attitude common in the public that government should solve all problems and provide for all needs. Communism, in spite of the official ideology, also left a "mentality" that work, initiative, and motivation are negative qualities. Both mentalities will require renovation if the societies are to become liberal, democratic societies.

"Democracy" means many different things to different people. Politicians especially are prone to attach to it a wide range of meanings, presumably to

TABLE 7
Failed States and their Foreign Policy, May–June 2006

Rank	Country	Mounting Demo-graphic Pressures	Massive Movement of Refugees and IDPs	Legacy of Vengence-Seeking Group Grievance	Chronic and Sustained Human Flight	Uneven Economic Develop-ment Along Group Lines	Sharp and/or Severe Economic Decline
35	Bosnia and Herze-govina	6.5	8.5	8.6	6	7.3	6.2
55	Serbia and Monte-negro	5.7	8.5	8.6	5.5	8	6.5
78	Macedo-nia	5.7	5.1	7.1	7	7.5	6
94	Albania	6	2.7	4.5	7	6	7
102	Romania	6.5	3.9	5.4	5.5	6	5.9
103	Bulgaria	6	4.1	4	6	6.2	4.3
104	Croatia	5.7	6.6	6.5	5	5.7	5.8
126	Slovenia	4	1.5	3.5	3.5	5.5	3.2

Source: Fund for Peace, www.fundforpeace.org. Washington, DC. Also Foreign Policy, May–June 2006,

serve their short-term purpose. In this study, an effort is made to operationalize the term in a way that offers utility and clarity. There is no suggestion here that any one conception is more accurate or intellectually superior. The definition provided in chapter 1 drawn from the IDEA study has appeal: "a system of political governance whose decision-making power is subject to the controlling influence of citizens who are considered political equals. A democratic system is inclusive, participatory, representative, accountable, transparent and responsive to citizens' aspirations and expectations." Our inventory differs a bit: here the defining elements of special import to transitional systems are tolerance, obligation, voice, constraint, transparency, and legitimacy. To reiterate, if we find these elements emerging in a transitional system, we should be comfortable calling it a democracy. As the region is examined, we find that effort toward these objectives is evident in fits and starts and is seldom coordinated. Policies and behaviors tug in opposite directions as rhetoric and practices di-

Criminal- ization or Delegitimi zation of the State	Progres- sive De- teriora- tion of Public Services	Wide- spread Violation of Human Rights	Security Apparatus as "State within a State"	Rise of Faction- alized Elites	Interven- tion of Other States or External Actors	Total	Net Change from 2005
8.1	5.8	5.3	7.5	8.7	10	88.5	5
7.8	5	5.6	6.5	8.6	7.5	83.8	−10.2
7.2	5.6	5.3	6.1	6.2	6.3	75.1	
7	6.9	5.5	5.5	4.5	6	68.6	
6.2	5.3	4.8	3.5	4.1	5.5	62.6	
6.2	5.3	4.9	5.5	4.1	5.5	62.1	
4.2	4.1	4.6	4	3.9	5.8	61.9	
3.2	3.5	3.7	3	1.2	1	36.8	

"Failed States Index," pp. 50–58.

verge and as specific policies clash. We acknowledged the various agents that play a role in the development of values and principles in these societies.

Establishing a value consensus as a "destination" for a democratic society is crucial. Designing and constructing a political machinery that can produce tangible results is a second task. Southeast Europe, like Central Europe before it, has the decided advantage of EU leadership in formatting such a political machinery. Leadership is also requisite to democratic development. The short-run dilemma is that neither "born-agains," nor "rookies" nor "imports" have demonstrated the elaborate skills needed for the job at hand. As a consequence, policy is hampered by a lack of confidence in those challenging areas where policy stability is the only hope of addressing a problem.

The notion that *tolerance* is the cornerstone value that must underpin a democratic system is supported with a multilevel case. Tolerance must operate in economics, religion, media, politics, ethnic, minority, and intellectual realms as well as in defining the community. We recognize that Southeast Europeans find it much easier to organize around what they are *against* rather than around what they are *for*. With that, we turn to the broad and methodologically impressive surveys done in recent years by and for the IDEA organization. These studies tell us that, overall, trust for institutions in the region is not automatic nor has the performance of governments yet earned it. Some 70 percent of the region's public does not believe that their respective countries are "run by the will of the people." Respondents pointed overwhelmingly to economic concerns when they think about either problems or "hopes." Violence, security, and a dysfunctional mentality are also mentioned prominently. Weighted just as heavily is the sense that the "solver" of all problems should be government. Some identify their own political establishment but many more see the EU as the knight in shining armor on the white horse. They also see structural political change as the means to solve problems.

In terms of their own role, citizens adamantly say that their only option is to participate in elections. In most cases, they are doing just that, and in large numbers—indeed, in such large numbers that it would appear that the elections have been corrupted. It is also reported that civil society is actually much weaker than it appears and is perceived broadly as marginal and ineffective (except in Croatia and Slovenia). The media suffers from an absence of trust and some structural and ownership problems of its own.

On the positive side of the ledger, surveys suggest that prejudice against groups (religious or ethnic) is localized. In many places, it is intense and politically formative but it would not appear to threaten to grip the region at large. Citizens apparently hold most executive political leaders in moderate to high esteem while seeing their political parties in a very negative light. The public believe that the provision of public services is inadequate, especially in the realm of social assistance or social welfare. They reflect extremely low levels of trust in virtually all political institutions. Only the Slovenes think they live in a democracy and the revealing and disturbing description of democracy that resonates is "democracy is freedom from any responsibility." In those areas where the international actors are engaged (Bosnia and Kosovo especially) democratic development itself is precluded by the political control and conduct of the international forces.

Southeast European political leaders have been prone to imagine themselves as trustees rather than delegates of the people. This self-image has conditioned them to drift from rather than toward democratic processes and policies. New constitutions in the region are met with skepticism. Bosnia and Kosovo "function" without constitutions and have shown signs that they will face a protracted struggle to create one. Sovereignty is yet another conundrum. Emerging from socialism, these countries claimed sovereignty to be a high priority. Yet with the realization of the challenges for small, independent countries in the twenty-first century, many are deliberately turning to the EU. Ironically, this shift will necessitate abandoning sovereignty in exchange for all the other benefits of the Union.

My study leads us to see that "voice" can be accommodated short of making policy. It asserts that the public must have a functional map (doors and windows) of the government in order to fulfill its role as participant. For that to be possible, the governmental design must have resolved in detail the centralization-decentralization issue; that is, who at what level is responsible for various functions. Elections cannot be the litmus test for establishing democracy in a society. Constituency issues, range of choices, amount of party pluralism, turnout, and political behavior between elections—all raise doubts about the value of elections as a singular indicator of democracy. IDEA adds still more issues to that list to underscore this caution.

The information landscape in Southeast Europe is complex and shows signs of vulnerability. Some small countries are media-saturated. Media outlets face cost-effectiveness assessments in both the public and commercial realms. They have also been hampered by "strategy-less" or "strategy-conflicted" international involvement with media enterprises. Political establishments are not clearly committed to pluralism in the media. Politicians still seem prone to see media as an asset for the opposition and a liability for the regime—despite the many cases of regime manipulation of the media. Comparative media analysts describe the atmosphere as "a fractured information environment." A few of Serbia's media companies seem the healthiest in the region.

Elections and voting systems highlight the mixed message from the region. The dominant electoral system is the proportional representation system that ensures a spectrum of representatives in proportion to the votes cast. It relies, however, heavily on the integrity of the political parties in each system (and as we know from the public opinion surveys, parties are held in very low esteem in the region). We know that the general public sees the elections as their primary avenue for participation. How then might they interpret the fact that more people register to vote than there are in the voting-age population?

We also know there is some distance to go before Southeast Europeans can rely on those in authority to accept the constraints required for democracy. Those in power must also find new and consistent respect for their counterparts in the opposition. The opposition, in turn, must also keep the broad public interest among their priorities. We know that transforming the legal system will require a legislative-executive partnership built around mutual respect. Those prone to violate the rules and engage in corrupt practices appear to be operating with more sophistication than their governmental counterparts. Economic transition may be the critical step to establishing political legitimacy— results, not words—and that will certainly require embracing a new culture.

Transparency in the region has cast bright light on the reality that the EU is actually prescribing many of the changes in both economics and politics. In essence, the Union is providing the value consensus (destination) necessary for democracy. We have acknowledged both that transparency must be a commitment made by all those in the system and that it nonetheless has limits that need be carefully defined. Even so, government must commit to assertive efforts to open its behavior to scrutiny, including issuing reports and exposing budgeting, committee deliberations, and policy-processing to interested investigators.

Legitimacy is complicated in Southeast Europe by the dramatic and ongoing value transition, by lack of governmental attention to this requisite, and by the untimely deaths of many of the central political figures in the region. Leadership turnover has created localized chaos in many systems and has so fundamentally changed policy courses that problems persist *because* of shifting policies. The loss or failure to establish legitimacy is most apparent in Bosnia, Kosovo, and Albania but it festers as a reality beneath the surface in Macedonia, Montenegro, and Serbia as well. Bulgaria and Romania may see emerging symptoms if they simply look more carefully at the texture of their own public's attitudes.

All this validates our diagnosis: Southeast Europe is in the midst of a transition that it only partially understands. It faces a range of challenges, primarily, how can the countries navigate their own journey when, in reality, the EU is the pilot? How can each maintain a robust identity without conceding that the ones who go it alone face decline? Democracy will require a fundamental transformation and take a generation to establish. Can the leadership develop the confidence to conclude that democracy is what the citizenry of the various regional countries actually want? Are elites and masses prepared or able to invest the energy to take on democratically required roles? Can politicians recreate their own images of themselves to embrace the more confining rules of democracy?

Prognoses

Let us presume for the moment the answer to most of these difficult questions is yes. The "destination" is democracy and market economy in the structured framework of the European Union. The prognosis for the health of these countries as they pursue that vision ranges from strong to dire. Slovenia has turned the corner and ensured its future. While healthy, it has challenges to address to remain the kind of player in the Union that it imagines itself. Croatia, Romania, and Bulgaria are a second cluster. Their problems are serious and their progress toward democracy is very mixed and conflicted. They have the capacity to be healthy but will need to make conscious and explicit decisions to improve their focus on democracy and to purge their systems of nagging qualities that can sabotage the journey toward their expressed destinations. These qualities may be understood as "disease" already inside the body that lurk and threaten health. Serbia, Montenegro, and Macedonia reveal greater problems: their negative dimensions already have a grip on those systems and more radical procedures will be required to exorcise the problems. Theirs is a more risky path given that priorities will naturally be controversial.

From a strict perspective on government performance, Bosnia, Kosovo, and Albania could be seen as comatose. Their fate, like that of the comatose patient, is in someone else's hands. They have little or no prospect of making themselves well. Only an emotional analysis could paint a bright prognosis for these systems. If they survive, it will only be by the benevolent and protracted engagement of external actors. But in this case, the textures of the system will not be democratic and the economy will not function by the market. It is time to issue prescriptions. The following list is a "Ten Commandments" of treatment to save the patient.

1. Recognize that strategies for development will be easier to maintain and much easier to explain to the political public if they are structured around the three broad requisites: coalesce a value consensus (common view of the destination); give explicit thought to the political architecture from which a political machinery will be assembled (enabling production of policies); and intensify the search for effective leaders (who embrace the democratic impulses and who are willing to take the society where it wants to go).

2. Explicitly frame for elites and masses alike an operational definition of "democracy." This analysis has determined the six requisites: tolerance, obligation, voice, constraint, transparency, and legitimacy but whatever elements are found meaningful in a specific system *must* become central to the public dialogue that forms around a democratic path.

3. Promote and reinforce tolerance at every opportunity. Elites must model tolerant behaviors. All institutions that model such behavior should be rewarded publicly and others should be brought before the court of public opinion.

4. Political parties and candidates should be required to address explicitly their perspectives on what has been defined here as "obligation." They should also commit publicly to any limits they see surrounding such a commitment.

5. Leadership must reassess any thinking that imagines "voice" as a problem to be managed. Instead, it must see voice as an essential and an asset to those in authority making public policy. For the mass public, voice is a responsibility to be prioritized and energized regularly.

6. Constraint requires the commitment to limit self-interest. It demands that politics be framed around precepts other than "we did it because we could." It is the normative essence of liberalism, the acceptance of respect for the latitude that individuals want left to them by government.

7. Transparency is a commitment to the faith that leadership must have in its public. The governed need to know. And the knowledge is more credible if less filtered. For democracy to function, both government and those actors outside of government need to embrace this standard.

8. Those in power must become very much more attuned to the centrality of legitimacy and how they can nurture it. It is the currency that can buy patience and accommodation from the political public in a system. A sense of legitimacy is especially important in transition or in times of systemic stress.

9. Because the Southeast European body politic is scarred by many unfortunate twists and turns in the lives and memories of their societies, it is critical that leadership recognize the realistic pace at which change can take root. Charisma and "plain talk" can begin to close the gap between expectations and real prospects for change. Politicians will need to summon courage in addressing such realities. Those in power will need to learn that criticism is a congenital feature of democracy.

10. The most important prescription is to recognize that democracy, although worthy above all else, is a goal that challenges every element of the body politic. It must be adapted and tuned to the rhythms of each particular society. It is neither friend nor foe. It is simply a flexible platform for people in society to craft a working relationship that minimizes exploitation and maximizes the pursuit of common goals.

Southeast Europeans may appropriately believe that they have the opportunity to learn about democracy from the rest of Europe and other established "democracies." We would do well to remember that we have much to learn from their experience. Their efforts to transition and frame a new system for themselves, give those living in "established democracies" a special opportunity to reconnoiter, rethink, and reexamine our thoughts about our own "democracy." A strong case can be made that we are due for a "checkup" that may expose our vulnerabilities. The freshness of the ideas in Southeast Europe can stimulate our willingness to remeasure our adherence to the ideals and practices of democracy.

Whose Model?

It has been my intention here to emphasize that the decisions regarding the architecture for the transitioning systems should be the responsibility (meant advisedly) of the countries themselves. It is their journey and their future. More explicitly, they are the ones who will live with the "destination" reflected in the value consensus that they must frame. They must agree to load onto the "bus" (political machinery) together to move expeditiously along the road toward their destination. And they are the ones who will choose (or, if not choose, tolerate) the leadership that will attempt to "drive" the bus toward the goals. Any number of circumstances can change the direction or sabotage the progress. For Southeast Europe, it may be that the greatest challenge is establishing a broad consensus on the destination. Political rhetoric in the region is rather clear: it touts democracy and the market as central objectives. Such rhetoric is reflected in the elite and mass articulations in the studies cited here. But what exactly those labels mean to the people who use them is a very different matter. The American model is of very limited use in Southeast Europe. It draws skepticism owing to the size and powerful economic platform that is the United States and has taken on extra problems of image through its aggressive and imposing foreign policy since the early 1990s. Political leaders in the region understand that replicating U.S. architecture for democracy is neither possible nor particularly desirable.

The variations of the European models seem much more relevant. The self-reflective and introspective processes associated with the evolution of the EU (ironically paralleling the timeframe of the transitions in Southeast Europe) have invited constructive interest in those developmental ideas. Though not our focus in this volume, the EU offers a decidedly different approach to "democracy." It has reengineered the architecture to streamline policymaking and has by design depended much more centrally on technocrats. The appeal of the European model(s) is not conceptual alone. Regimes in the region under study here—except perhaps for Serbia—have found the European policies (both foreign and domestic) and political mechanisms more palatable and the resource commitment to nurture such changes in Southeast Europe more forthcoming.

My design here was to broaden the vision, provide a generic definition of value-reflecting goals common to "democracy," and to prescribe steps that create movement toward a system that is sustainable and broadly people-focused (that is, liberal in the classic sense). It is assuredly the domain of every system to find the special texture of its own democracy. In that search, it is important to recognize the quite common contradictions and missteps that occur. The transition is made more complex by a narrow time frame and by external meddling that presumes to understand the Southeast European environment. The Dayton Accords and the 180-degree reversal in U.S. and U.N. positions on Kosovar independence are two prominent examples of the latter. Both have become major inhibitors to democratic development in the region. The twenty-first century is a time of keen competitiveness and the new systems in Southeast Europe have no choice but to acknowledge that they will need to compete with other states in the marketplace and in world affairs. More important is the reality that their publics, given our information-saturated world, will see the experience of other countries and will necessarily measure their lives and their governments against the others they see around them and around the world. This global vision heightens the challenge of all transitional systems.

.   .   .

"Don't happy; Be worry" is the cryptic song title of the irreverent pop singer/star Rambo Amadeus. It is the root message reflecting the caution with which Southeast Europeans approach anyone purporting to bring "solutions." If the ideas presented here provoke more debate, if they generate some discussion, if they nurture a realistic caution about the path—democratic or otherwise—toward the future of Southeast Europe, they shall have proved worthwhile.

Notes

Chapter 1. The Balkans (pages 4–23)

1. Aleksander Stipcevic, ed. *The Illyrians* (Park Ridge, N.J.: Noyes, Publishers, 1977); John Wilkes, Barry Cunliffe, and James Campbell, eds. *The Illyrians: Peoples of Europe* (London: Blackwell, 1995).
2. It is perhaps useful to think of these methods as early forms of revenue generation for a political system—a kind of free-form customs or duty.
3. Aluise Zorzi, *Venice: A City, A Republic, An Empire* (New York: Overlook. 2001); Jan Morris, *The Venetian Empire: A Sea Voyage* (New York: Penguin, 1990); David Nicolle, and Christopher Rothero, *The Venetian Empire, 1200–1670* (Westminster, Md.: Osprey, 1989).
4. Daniel Kaufmann, Aart Kray, and Massimo Mastruzzi, *Governance Matters IV: Indicators for 1996–2004* (Washington, D.C.: World Bank Institute, 2005).
5. "What is Democracy?" International Institute for Democracy and Electoral Assistance, http:// www.idea.int/democracy/index.cfm?renderfor print=1&, p. 1.
6. Ibid.
7. IDEA Handbook on Democracy Assessment, http://www.idea.int/democracy/sod .cfm?renderfor print=1&.
8. Ibid.
9. Ibid.
10. Ibid.

Chapter 2. Tolerance (pages 24–39)

1. Drago Hedl, "Free Trade Plan Alarms Croats," *Balkan Insight no. 20*, February 9, 2006, Balkan Investigative Reports Network, www.birn.eu.com; "Croatians Cool to Idea of Balkan Free-Trade Zone," *RFE/RL Newsline*, February 1, 2006, part 2, vol. 10, no. 19, www.rferl.org/newsline; "Serbia's Agriculture Minister Comes Out in Support of Free Trade Zone," *RFE/RL Newsline*, February 6, 2006, part 2, vol. 10, no. 22, www.rferl.org/newsline; "Croatian, Albanian Prime Ministers Talk about Expanding Free Trade," *RFE/RL Newsline*, February 28, 2006, part 2, vol. 10, no. 37, www.rferl.org/newsline.
2. Miroslav Zadrepko, "Serbian Church Claims Victim Status," *Balkan Insight 17*, January 20, 2006, Balkan Investigative Reports Network, www.birn.eu.com; "Serbian Orthodox Church Complains of Harrassment," *RFE/RL Newsline*, January 23, 2006, part 2, vol. 10, no. 12, www.rferl.org/newsline.
3. Ibid.
4. Ivan Blazevski and Zelimir Bojaovic, "Serbia Financing Rival Macedonian Church," *Balkan Insight 27*, March 27, 2006, Balkan Investigative Reports Network, www.birn.eu.com.

5. Ibid.

6. A "fundamentalist state" is a political system that "aims directly at the reconstruction of temporal power for religious organizations and their leaders. It denies the separation of the religious sphere from all other spheres and especially from the political, social, and cultural domains. Fundamentalism affirms the supremacy of the religious sphere over all others and the supremacy of its interpreters over all other socio-political actors. It claims that religious criteria must be not only the dominant but the exclusive arbiter of behavior," *The Oxford Companion to Politics of the World* (Oxford: Oxford University Press, 1993), 820.

7. Tamara Causidis and Boris Georgievski, "In Depth: Macedonian Media in Disarray," *Balkan Insight 26,* March 18, 2006, Balkan Investigative Reports Network, www.birn.eu.com.

8. BBC. "President Apologizes over Croatian War," September 10, 2003 (Stipe Mesic [Croatian president] makes speech in Belgrade articulating regret for behaviors during Yugoslav civil war in Slavonia).

9. Tim Judah, *Kosovo: War and Revenge* (New Haven: Yale University Press, 2002); *The Serbs: History, Myths and the Destruction of Yugoslavia* (New Haven: Yale University Press, 2000).

10. Richard Farkas, "State-Building and the Final Status of Kosovo," in *Democratic Development and Political Terrorism: The Global Perspective* (Boston: Northeastern University Press), 420–454.

11. Tim Judah, "Kosovo: Countdown to Independence," *Balkan Insight 21,* February 16, 2006, Balkan Investigative Reports Network, www.birn.eu.com; "Serbian Premier Calls on Citizens to Defend Kosovo," *RFE/RL Newsline,* January 8, 2007, part 2, vol. 11, no. 3, www.rferl.org/newsline; "Macedonian President Warns of Possible Kosova Instability," *RFE/RL Newsline,* January 25, 2007, part 2, vol. 11, no. 15, www.rferl.org/newsline; "NATO Chief Warns Violence in Kosova Could have Domino Effect," *RFE/RL Newsline,* January 31, 2007, part 2, vol. 11, no. 19, www.rferl.org/newsline; "Kosovar-Serb Leader Warns of War Sooner or Later," *RFE/RL Newsline.* February 2, 2007, part 2, vol. 11, no. 21, www.rferl.org/newsline; "New Kosovar President Says Independence Non-Negotiable," *RFE/RL Newsline,* February 13, 2006, part 2, vol. 10, no. 27, www.rferl.org/newsline; "Serbian President's Proposed 20 Year Wait on Kosovoa's Status Gets Cool Reception in Security Council," *RFE/RL Newsline,* February 15, 2006, part 2, vol. 10, no. 29, www.rferl.org/newsline.

12. Nikola Lazic, "Partition Demand Fuels South Serbia Tensions," *Balkan Insight 21,* February 16, 2006, Balkan Investigative Reports Network, www.birn.eu.com. See also: *Reporting Ethnic Minority Issues,* British Association for Central and Eastern Europe, November 2006, http://www.bacee.orguk/projects.asp; "Albanians in South Serbia Adopt Proposal for Autonomy," *RFE/RL Newsline,* January 10, 2006, part 2, vol. 10, no. 4, www.rferl.org/newsline; "Serbian Plan Seeks Autonomy for Three Kosovar Regions," *RFE/RL Newsline,* January 11, 2006, part 2, vol. 10, no. 5, www.rferl.org/newsline; "Kosova's Parliamentary Speaker Rejects Establishment of Serbian Entity in Province," *RFE/RL Newsline,* January 12, 2006, part 2, vol.10, no. 6, www.rferl.org/newsline; "Bosnian Politician Says Kosovar Serbs Might be

Moved to Republika Srpska," *RFE/RL Newsline,* January 10, 2007, part 2, vol. 11, no. 5, www.rferl.org/newsline.

13. Tamara Causidis and Maja Ivanovska, "Roma Scorn Their On-Screen Portrayal." *Balkan Insight 21,* February 16, 2006, Balkan Investigative Reports Network, www.birn.eu.com.

14. Ivan Blazevski, "Macedonia: Reworked History Lessons Cause Storm," *Balkan Insight 20,* February 9, 2006, Balkan Investigative Reports Network, www.birn.eu .com. Also: the Centre for South East European Studies at http://www.csees.net/ ?page=country_analysis&country_id=5&ca_id=2089.

15. Aida Sunje, "Turkish Students Take Refuge in Sarajevo," *Balkan Insight 23,* March 3, 2006, Balkan Investigative Reports Network, www.birn.eu.com.

Chapter 3. Obligation (pages 40–57)

1. Gordana Katana, "Dodik Hostage to his Own Promises," *Balkan Insight 21,* February 16, 2006, Balkan Investigative Reports Network, www.birn.eu.com.

2. Ibid.

3. IDEA Southeastern Europe surveys: Gallup and PULS, *South-Eastern Europe and the Stability Pact: New Means for Regional Analysis CROATIA* (Zagreb: PULS), March 2001; Gallup and PULS, *South-Eastern Europe and the Stability Pact: New means for Regional Analysis FEDERATION OF BOSNIA AND HERCEGOVINA. Sarajevo: PULS,* March 2001; Forum: Center for Strategic Research and Documentation, *Balkan Public Agenda* (Skopje: Forum), June 2001; Vitosha Research, *Balkan Public Agenda: Sofia and Cherna Gora* (Sofia: Vitosha), February 2000; *Balkan Public Agenda: Kosova* (Prishtine: Gallup), May 2001; SMMRI Group, *Balkan Public Agenda: Republic of Srpska* [Bosnia-Hercegovina] (Banja Luka: SMMRI), January 2001; SMMRI Group, *Balkan Public Agenda: Serbia* (Belgrade: SMMRI), February 2001; SMMRI Group, *Balkan Public Agenda: Montenegro* (Podgorica: SIMMRI), February 2001.

4. Ibid.

5. Nevena Angelovska, "Macedonian Smokers Say Health Drive is a Drag," *Balkan Insight 15,* January 14, 2006, Balkan Investigative Reports Network, www.birn .eu.com.

6. Nidzara Ahmetasevic, "Debate Follows Collapse of Bosnia Reform Drive," *Balkan Insight 20,* February 9, 2006, Balkan Investigative Reports Network, www .birn.eu.com.

7. Ibid.

8. Ibid.

9. Ibid.

10. Ibid.

11. Tatyana Dimitrova, "EU Focus: Bulgaria Rushes EU Agricultural Reforms," *Balkan Insight 26,* March 18, 2006, Balkan Investigative Reports Network. www.birn.eu.com. Also of interest: "Serbian President Says EU Candidacy Top Serbian Goal for 2007," *RFE/RL Newsline,* January 3, 2007, part 2, vol. 11, no. 1, www.rferl.org/newsline.

Chapter 4. Voice (pages 58–78)

1. Marian Chiriac, "Autonomy Call Raises Romanian Hackles," *Balkan Insight 26,* March 18, 2006, Balkan Investigative Reports Network, www.birn.eu.com.
2. Marcus Tanner, "Dash for Statehood Leaves Some Montenegrins Cold," *Balkan Insight 24,* March 10, 2006, Balkan Investigative Reports Network. www.birn .eu.com. Of related interest: "Montenegrin Premier Presses on With Referendum Despite Threat of Boycott," *RFE/RL Newsline,* January 4, 2006, part 2, vol. 10, no. 1, www.rferl.org/newsline.
3. Ibid.
4. Ibid.
5. Zelimir Bojovic and Dragana Nikolic-Solomon, "In Depth: Serbia Promises Mladic Action Plan," *Balkan Insight 20,* February 9, 2006, Balkan Investigative Reports Network, www.birn.eu.com.
6. Thom Shanker, "Aftereffects: Rebuilding; Lessons for Iraq Seen in Balkan Aftermath," *New York Times,* May 22, 2003, final late edition, sec. A, p. 15.
7. http://www.idea.int/Europe_cis/index.cfm?renderfor print=1&.
8. Ibid.
9. Estimates by Transparency International use "market prices" and calculate that for a fifteen-day period parties and candidates spent at least €1.5 million far in excess of the legal limits. They also suggest that "true" costs have been regularly "buried."
10. Nevana Angelovska, "Macedonian Election Expenses in the Spotlight," *Balkan Insight 20,* March 3, 2006, Balkan Investigative Reports Network, www.birn .eu.com.
11. Ibid.
12. Drawn from a composite of international donor organizations. One Dutch source, media expert Yasha Lange (executive secretary of the Media Task Force) estimates the total nearer to €250 million. Speech: "Stability Pact for South Eastern Europe," http://www.stabilitypact.org/wt1/040607-speech.asp.
13. Nerma Jelacic, Aida Sunje, and Ilda Zornic, "Poor Donor Strategy Doomed Projects in Bosnia," *Balkan Insight 19,* February 6, 2006, Balkan Investigative Reports Network, www.birn.ec.com. The media in Bosnia received far more in foreign donations than their counterparts in Serbia and Croatia. Owing to a lack of coordination, however, they have achieved less.
14. Nermin Durmo, former chairman of the Bosnia and Hercegovina (BiH) Press Council emphasizes that international donors engaged themselves in BiH without understanding the media or political environment in former Yugoslavia. See: *Article 19: Global Campaign for Free Expression,* Conference Report on Freedom and Accountability: Conference on Media Self-Regulation in Southeast Europe, Sarajevo, 2005 (London), 1–24.
15. Nerma Jelacic, et al. (see note 13, this chapter).
16. Ibid.
17. Daniel Lindvall, "Imposed Reform Facing Its Ultimate Test," *Balkan Insight 19,* February 8, 2006, Balkan Investigative Reports Network. www.birn.eu.com. His

analysis underscores that a late start and inconsistent support have neutralized the reform of Bosnia's public broadcasting system.

18. Antoaneta Arsova, "Bulgaria's Private Media in Jeopardy," *Balkan Insight 15,* January 14, 2006, Balkan Investigative Reports Network, www.birn.eu.com.

19. Per Byman, "Comment: Evaluating our Efforts." *Balkan Insight 19,* February 7, 2006, Balkan Investigative Reports Network, www.birn.eu.com.

20. In a "List Proportional Representation" (List PR) system, each party or grouping presents a list of candidates for a multimember electoral district, the voters vote for a party, and parties receive seats in proportion to their overall share of the vote.

21. A "Mixed Member Proportional" system is one in which the choices expressed by the voters are used to elect representatives through two different systems—one List PR system and one plurality/majority system—where the List PR system compensates for the disproportionality in the results of the plurality/majority system.

Chapter 5. Constraint (pages 79–88)

1. "Serbia Issues Arrest Warrant for Telecom Boss Over Kosova Deal," *RFE/RL Newsline,* January 4, 2006, part 2, vol. 10, no. 1. www.rferl/newsline.org; "Serbian Central Banker Arrested for Alleged Bribery." *RFE/RL Newsline,* January 13, 2006, part 2, vol. 10, no. 7, www.rferl/newsline.org; "Tycoon Says Serbian Government Persecuting Him for Political Reasons," *RFE/RL Newsline,* January 13, 2006, part 2, vol. 10, no. 7, www.rferl/newsline.org; Tanja Matic, "Serbia Declares War on Phone Tycoon," *Balkan Insight 16,* January 14, 2006, Balkan Investigative Reports Network, www.birn.eu.com; "Top Serbian Businessman Charged with Fraud, Tax Evasion," *RFE/RL Newsline,* January 17, 2006, part 2, vol. 10, no. 8, www.rferl/ newsline.org; "Judge Orders Detention for Serbian Central Bank Offical in Bribery Case," *RFE/RL Newsline,* January 17, 2006, part 2, vol. 10, no. 8, www.rferl/ newsline.org; "Serbian Justice Minister Defends Government's Anticorruption Moves," *RFE/RL Newsline,* January 17, 2006, part 2, vol. 10, no. 8, www.rferl/ newsline.org; "Arrest Warrant Issued for Indicted Former Serbian Telecom Boss." *RFE/RL Newsline,* January 18, 2006, part 2, vol. 10, no. 9, www.rferl/newsline.org; "As Tycoon-Politician Slams Serbian Government," *RFE/RL Newsline,* January 18, 2006, part 2, vol. 10, no. 9, www.rferl/newsline.org; "MOBTEL Executive Arrested in Belgrade," *RFE/RL Newsline,* January 25, 2006, part 2, vol. 10, no. 14, www .rferl/newsline.org; "Serbia Files Tax-Evasion Charges Against Karić Brothers," *RFE/RL Newsline,* February 8, 2006, part 2, vol. 10, no. 24, www.rferl/newsline.org.

Chapter 6. Transparency (pages 89–99)

1. Arbana Xharra, "Kosovars Seek Compensation," *Balkan Insight 16,* January 14, 2006, Balkan Investigative Reports Network, www.birn.eu.com.

2. Richard Farkas, "State-Building and the Final Status of Kosovo," in *Democratic Development and Political Terrorism: The Global Perspective* (Boston: Northeastern University Press, 2005), 420–454.

3. Jasper Dick, "Comment: Privatisation Remains Central to Kosovo's Economic Revival," *Balkan Insight 27,* April 1, 2006, Balkan Investigative Reports Network, www.birn.eu.com. Dick Jasper is managing director of the Kosovar Trust Agency, which manages all privatizations.

4. Nedjelko Rudovic, "Montenegrins Fear Crackdown on State Broadcaster," *Balkan Insight 17,* January 20, 2006, Balkan Investigative Reports Network, www.birn.eu.com.

5. Ibid. A position championed by the Association of Young Journalists in Montenegro.

6. International Research and Exchange Board (IREX). *Media Sustainability Index 2005* (New York: IREX, 2005), 43.

Chapter 7. Legitimacy (pages 100–108)

1. Tim Judah is the author of two recent volumes on Kosovar political affairs. Milazim Krasniqi, "LDK Leaders Jostle for Rugova's Crown," *Balkan Insight 18,* January 27, 2006, Balkan Investigative Reports Network, www.birn.eu.com; Arben Qirezi, "Line-up of Possible Successors," *Balkan Insight 18,* January 27, 2006, Balkan Investigative Reports Network, www.birn.eu.com; Vladimir Sudar, "Serbs Fear Rugova's Radical Heirs," *Balkan Insight 18,* January 27, 2006, Balkan Investigative Reports Network, www.birn.eu.com; Marcus Tanner, "Man of Letters Who Led Independence Struggle," *Balkan Insight 18,* January 27, 2006, Balkan Investigative Reports Network, www.birn.eu.com; Tim Judah, "Architect of a Separate Kosovo Dies," *Balkan Insight 18,* January 27, 2006, Balkan Investigative Reports Network, www.birn.eu.com; Zana Limani, "Kosovo Ditches its Prime Minister," *Balkan Insight 23,* March 3, 2006, Balkan Investigative Reports Network, www.birn.eu.com; "Kosovo's President Dies, Leaving Leadership Void," *RFE/RL Newsline,* January 23, 2006, part 2, vol. 10, no. 12, www.rferl/newsline.org; Patrick Moore, "Kosovo After Rugova," *RFE/RL Newsline,* January 23, 2006, part 2, vol. 10, no. 12, www.rferl/newsline.org; idem., "Rugova and his Legacy," *RFE/RL Newsline,* January 27, 2006, part 2, vol. 10, no. 16, www.rferl/newsline.org.

Other regional leaders who died leaving new pressures include Trajkovski (Macedonia) and Marjanovic (Serbia). See: "Late Macedonia Presidnt's Brother Says Case Not Closed in Fatal Plane Crash," *RFE/RL Newsline,* February 27, 2006, part 2, vol. 10, no. 36, www.rferl.newsline.org; "Former Serbian Prime Minister Dies," *RFE/RL Newsline,* February 23, 2006, part 2, vol. 10, no. 34, www.rferl/newsline.org.

2. Andi Balla, "EU Focus: Albanians Frustrated by Long Road to Brussels," *Balkan Insight 20,* February 9, 2006, Balkan Investigative Reports Network, www.birn.eu.com; "NATO Tells Albania that Fair Elections Cricual to Membership Hopes," *RFE/RL Newsline,* January 11, 2007, part 2, vol. 11, no. 6, www.rferl/newsline.org; "EU Welcomes Albanian Election Compromise," *RFE/RL Newsline,* January 18, 2007, part 2, vol. 11, no. 10, www.rferl/newsline.org.

3. Nidzara Ahmetasevic, "VAT Adds to Burden on Bosnia's Poor," *Balkan Insight 17,* January 20, 2006, Balkan Investigative Reports Network, www.birn.eu.com.

4. Quote from Marko Vicinic reported by Dragana Nikolic-Solomon, and Vladimir Sudar, "Democratic Party Boosts Tadić's Hand," *Balkan Insight 22,* February 23, 2006, Balkan Investigative Reports Network, www.birn.eu.com.

Chapter 8. Prescription for a Badly Scarred Body Politic (pages 109–122)

1. Daniel Kaufmann, Aart Kray, and Massimo Mastruzzi. *Governance Matters IV: Indicators for 1996–2004* (Washington, D.C.: World Bank Institute, 2005).

Index